The Body Burden

Living in the Shadow of Barbie

The Body Burden

Living in the Shadow of Barbie

Stacey Handler

Certain names have been changed to protect privacy.

Blue Note Publications, Inc.
110 Polk Avenue, Suite 3
Cape Canaveral, FL 32920
1-800-624-0401

ISBN 1-878398-21-0
Library of Congress Control Number: 00-131731

Dover graphics used by permission:
Desk-Gallery Mega-Bundle © 1995 Dover Publications, and Zedcor, Inc.
Cover painting of woman by Elliot Handler
Cover design by Paul Maluccio

www.bodyburden.com

Printed in the United States of America

This book is dedicated to my mother Suzie, my sister Samantha, my brother Jeff, and my grandparents Ruth and Elliot Handler.

A special dedication to the one man I could always count on: Thanks, Dad, for guiding my hands through some very difficult pages. The lessons you've taught me will always live on in my words.

Acknowledgments

A special thanks to Beverly Anderson, Paul Maluccio, Dr. Susan Barron and my mother Suzie, for their continuous help and support on this project. And a special thanks to my dog Max, who sat up keeping me company through all those long nights on the computer and whose snuggling and kisses kept me going through the difficult times.

A special thanks to my grandfather for the priceless contribution of his wonderful artwork.

His paintings have taken their quiet place on many of our family walls and I am glad that I was able to bring them out of hiding and into these heartfelt pages.

Elliot Handler

Table of Contents

Introduction

Ken is my father, Barbie is my aunt, and the less-well-known Stacie doll was named after me. My grandparents are the original founders of the Mattel toy company, and my grandmother was the creator of the Barbie doll. Other than that, life is pretty ordinary. Of course, there are a few exceptions, the main one being the irony of my own problems with body image. The real-life Stacie doll types these pages in between strange eating habits and skipped meals.

It is easy to say that Barbie has had nothing to do with women deciding to have breast implants or starve themselves to death. It is also just as easy to put all the blame on her. Unfortunately, there has been so much emphasis on blame that the real issues about this larger-than-life icon have become an argument for the media.

I do not believe that my grandmother had any idea how Barbie would take the world by storm; if she were still in the driver's seat, I believe there would be "heavy" Barbie and Stacie dolls on the market today. The question is: Would the majority of the population buy them? Therein lies the problem. So Barbie lovers can rest easy; Barbie is not to blame, we are. As a society, we buy into this perfect image that has been placed as a mental burden on the shoulders of women everywhere.

Okay, here it goes—my true attempt at explaining how it feels to be part of the family that created the Barbie doll. First of all, there is a tremendous amount of guilt that I carry around. After all, why should somebody in my position complain at all about Barbie? She is the main source of my income and security. Since I am not the money-making type and I have lived my life as an artist, I should be thanking Barbie for the money that my grandparents have generously given me over the years.

I am very happy about my financial situation and money has bought me a lot. I have more CDs than I know what to do with. I have a nice Manhattan apartment with a view of the Chrysler building and my own home gym. But as I do my final bicep curl at two in the morning, I realize with great sadness that there is one thing money hasn't bought me—a self-image that I can live with.

So, yes, there is some guilt when I complain about Barbie, but the guilt stops here. It has not been easy being the granddaughter of the woman who created Barbie. Most young girls have an option about how much of the Barbie ideal they have to contend with. I never wanted a Barbie doll in my life, but that doll and her perfect image stared me in the face frequently enough to give anyone a body-image and/or eating-disorder problem.

I never played with dolls when I was a child. I grew up watching *Charlie's Angels* and I looked up to them very much, the way many little girls looked up to their dolls. It was very confusing to grow up thinking that average women could actually look like that and be real people. They looked so much like the doll Grandma had created that I believed it was possible for any woman to be both the perfect doll and a real person. Imagine my disappointment when my body failed the test.

What led me to overeat had a lot to do with my having diabetes, and although my parents were not overly restrictive about diet, other people always treated me differently. I always felt as if I had to take more before someone would come and take it away from me.

So I grew up thinking that everybody else could have

that ice cream sundae, but that I couldn't. Even though I now know differently, and I've seen that most people cannot eat whatever they want, the child inside me still feels the need to make sure I get a treat—that I won't get cheated. It was rough living with diabetes as a teenager, with Barbie's perfect image hanging over me.

Barbie represented success to my grandmother and as a young child, I felt that my body represented failure to her. This feeling continued as I grew into a young woman: Why did my tummy stick out so much that I couldn't wear a bikini? Why was I so fat? Why did I need to feel guilty after every meal that wasn't "baby" size?

I've been told that I have a beautiful and shapely body, but when the sickness takes over, I don't believe it. Even when I have lost a lot of weight, the sickness of an unattainable perfection lingers over me like a cloud of black smoke after a fire.

So, I am happy not to be struggling financially, but for me to deny my feelings about "living in the shadow of Barbie" would be untrue and unfair, both to myself and to my readers. In fact, if anyone has the right to complain about Barbie, it is I. However, that is not what this book is about.

Barbie has been a large part of the reason for my body-image downfall, but that does not mean that she is the cause of everybody else's body-image problem; it is more what her icon represents that is the problem. Whether it be Cindy Crawford, Pamela Anderson, Twiggy, or even Barbie whom women view as the perfect icon is irrelevant. Whether or not it is subconsciously felt, these images of the perfect body are what women have been forced to look at every day on billboards, TV commercials, and so much more.

My problems are magnified because Barbie has been a part of my family all my life. I am an artist at heart, and as such I do not hate the mere creation of her. It is how her existence has followed me through my own traumas with food and body image that makes this enough of an irony to fill these pages.

True, these words are for the most part autobiographical, but they reach out to women everywhere. So even though these are my very personal feelings, they are universal as well. I have chosen to write a section about anorexia and bulimia because I have spent so many hours, daily, suffering over my body. So besides having poetic license, I feel very close to anybody who has suffered an eating disorder. I know that if I weren't so repulsed by vomiting, I would be hugging my share of toilets.

Being in the Barbie-doll family has had its good moments, as well as its bad. I now know that I am so much more than the sum of my grandmother's successes and failures. I am a person who will not be defined by the measurements of a doll. I am a survivor; I have survived, and will continue to survive, my body-image disorder.

If this book helps one woman to realize that she is not alone in this never-ending battle for perfection, then this mission of hope was well worth the effort.

Let me take you inside
to where the food goes,
and I hide...

The Hidden Voice

A lot of women feel powerless and afraid to find their own individual voice. So they end up using food (or lack of it) to compensate for the hidden voice that is buried deep within them.

If Barbie suddenly became a real person, she might very well have a hidden voice, different from the one society has given her. However, the fact that she cannot speak leaves women and young girls with a message that society has continued to send, through the media and the fashion industry. Society tends to forget about individual people and their feelings.

On and Off the Shelves

I sit on the shelves
so perfectly put together,
not an ounce of makeup smudged.

My pretty dresses
on my very pretty body
can sometimes be sold separately.

I am an inspiration
for so many hopeful children,
the first grown-up doll
to really show them what they can be.

I am played with—
tossed around—
from one parent's shopping cart to the next
until I finally find peace in a child's eyes.

The children see me looking my best,
taking over almost every toy store,
and because of brilliant advertising
they always come back for more.

They never see behind the curtains
that hide all my imperfections,
the times when I am sad,
depressed,
when I can't always look my best,

like the time I opened an ice cream store,
gained weight from too many peppermint cones.
I was removed from the shelves
where the perfect me of the former year
remained without a single tear.

I worked day and night
to get rid of my excess cellulite
until I looked like myself again,
perfect in the eyes of society.

I've been black.
I've even been a brunette.
I've been everything
but heavyset.

I work every day,
making lots of money.
Boy do I pay!

If a pound comes on,
I am scolded,
told to work harder
until my brain turns to flab.
I become no smarter.

Bleached in the sun,
everybody's dream of beauty;
there are so many dreams I have.

Dreams are really hidden opportunities
that follow us throughout our lives
but, as the perfect body follows me,
there is so much more I want to be.

Sometimes I want to be real—
a real woman—
because I am not.

I am plastic,
unrealistic,
tired inside
from the long days on the treadmill
with nowhere really to run.

Real women can run the longest mile,
win the race by just being beautiful inside.
Society gave me my body;
don't let it give you yours.

Steven Cavallo

Unheard and Hungry

Me at sixteen

The Shell

You look so lost.
Can't you find me?

I am over here
inside the shell,
the protective layers around me.

Please come search for me.
I promise, I am under here somewhere.
I need to come out,
but I am afraid,

afraid to open the curtains,
afraid of what I might find,
that you might be waiting for me
and that I will be naked.

Exposed to emotion
shoved inside with so many forks.
Will you be able to see inside
or will I be merely fog to your searching eyes?

Will you make me open up to you?
And if you do,
how will it feel?

It's been so long since I've cried
or laughed, and meant it.
My fat has sheltered me
from fingers that tickle.

Come into my shell.
I need to feel your hands
all over me like blankets of rain.

Come in where I've kept myself warm;
see where all the food has gone
into the hole
that I've never really been able to fill.

Come see the desert inside me,
the sand of all my uncried tears,
the trees that kept me from being burned.

Hold me while I cry;
let me know I am safe
to show you who I am
and that you have fears too.

If I let you find my secret places,
if I become myself like never before,
will you rock me to sleep
until I am just a baby in your arms?

Will you love me completely,
knowing that I am incomplete,
unable to love myself sometimes?

I am here.
Come find me.

Let me take you inside
to where the food goes,
and I hide.

Marriage made me silent. Silence made me eat. One day the silence exploded and became the loudest noise I'd ever heard. My marriage was over. I had just begun to live.

Steven Cavallo

Silence

The anger tastes bitter
as each bite of food goes into my mouth.
I just want to be heard.
Why is there so much silence?

Would you just hear me,
change your rigid opinions,
stop abusing me,
telling me how stupid I am?

I will change you
after I finish this one last splurge.
I will make you treat me nice
after I fulfill this one last urge.

I will tell you off
after I watch my soaps on the tube,
after I dive inside my fantasy
that dinner will make my pain go away.

I will let you know once and for all
how much you've hurt me,
demolished my self-esteem—
as soon as I have my cookies and ice cream.

I guess I will have to leave you
right after I make us just one more dinner,
after all the love is cooked out
and I die inside once more.

I woke up one day in the midst of a verbally abusive marriage and layers of fat that numbed my reality.

Fortunately, I didn't succumb to such an unworthy fate. I found my true self waiting at the other side of divorce. I found my own self-worth, and I am convinced that my marriage was a blessing in disguise. To truly find ourselves, sometimes we need to walk through our own self-delusions.

1998—185 pounds.

What If I Were to Tell You?

What if I were to tell you
that I am what I am,
that you cannot change me,
mold me,
lessen my integrity?

What if I just happen to mention
that I am just as beautiful as anybody,
even though I am not a cliché clone of society?

Have I mentioned lately
how intruded on I've felt,
allowing myself to be clay
for people's molding hands?
The statue has broken;
I have broken out.

Have I told all of you
the changes you should make?

No, I suppose I haven't,
because if I had,
I would see
I cannot change you either.

You have your faults,
flaws that I trip on whenever you tell me
that I should do something different with my life—
eat healthier,
become more involved in everyday routine.

Have I mentioned my new consciousness,
my realization
that food is my teddy bear,
not anybody else's to tell me
how not to embrace it?

Have I told you lately
how hurt you make me feel,
how angry I am
to be a part of your trivial discussions,
matters that should remain private,
and opinions about everybody but yourselves?

Can you please try
accepting a beautiful person as they are,
not expecting them to be the image
of what you think they should be?

Have I mentioned
how much love I know you have for me?
I love you too,
but I love you freely.
Scars can show and I will kiss them,
not erase them with new instructions for living.

Can you all find it within yourselves
to love me freely
with all my eccentricity,
extra pounds,
unearthly habits?

Have I mentioned lately
that I will love you anyway,
even though you hurt me?
I will love you despite yourselves,
the parts of you that are also inadequate.

I've been suffocated by your ideas.
Let me breathe again.
Let me be myself,
eat French fries
without being railroaded to a nutritionist.

Let me live,
or I will die unknown,
to me.

Food for Comfort

Married to McDonald's

Lost my man
when he caught me immersed
in my Big Mac and fries,
my world of hunger and thirst.

He couldn't accept
my attraction to the Quarter Pounder;
he wanted me to live in his world
of salmon and flounder,

dry on my plate,
no pickles and sauce.
Had to have it his way,
had to be the boss.

I became bored,
felt depleted and ignored,
so I accepted Mickey D's
abundant award.

It felt like magic
nights of beautiful sex;
my man couldn't understand,
so he became my ex.

He couldn't watch
as I ate my fries;
as they melted in my mouth,
something melted between my thighs.

I took my vows
when all was said and done,
in sickness and in health—
with or without the bun.

Hello, My Name Is Stacey I Am an Overeater

Hello,
my name is Stacey.
I am an overeater.

Food has always been there for me;
it never judges me;
it fills me when I need filling;
it represents every dare I never dared.

It is the perfect end to a bad day,
the perfect light at the end of darkness,
the dream that sweeps my nightmares away,
the hand I hold when I'm afraid.

What am I so afraid of?
Life, I guess,
or just living in such a vast universe.
Food keeps me hidden.

I hide in front of the television
where soap operas are the world I see,
where everybody looks perfect;
the real world isn't like that.

Still sometimes I forget
that the real world has real people
and I am lost once again in my food
and the fantasy.

Food keeps me outside of life
like a child
with its nose pressed against a candy store window.
Growing up is scary.

Food is the perfect friend,
the loving companion on a lonely night,
the perfect sensual experience
where taste buds become like genitals.

I guess what I'm trying to say
is that I love food
but I am sad
because it can't love me back.

Daisy's Diet Disaster

There's a light burning in the kitchen,
an egg frying in the pan,
a flame flaming on the stove,
some sushi from Japan.

There's a light burning in the bedroom,
a TV shining bright;
since I have no date,
I just lick the plate.

Funny how the moon is made of cheese
and when I look in the mirror,
I see Dom Deluise.
Bananas and cream are my latest passion;
it's absurd to carry on in this fashion.

I look out my window to see the stars.
Oh, heavens!
I only see Snicker's bars.

It's such a pity,
such a waste,
that everything I touch must have a taste.
Even you tasted of sugar and spice.
Now your crumbs are all gone,
eaten by the mice.

There's a light burning in the kitchen,
a growling pain in my tummy.
It's almost 3 a.m.;
how I long for something yummy.

There's always food in the 'fridge,
some leftover wine—
wine left from so long ago
when we used to dine.

We dined together way back when,
when life was a diet.
We danced through the night,
made love until dawn,
but you never could keep my stomach quiet.

So when you come back around,
there will be no mistaking:
I have no time for love,
only my baking.

No time for diets,
so boring and plain.
What I eat for love
keeps away the pain.

Me at 19—
One of those rare moments when I appreciated my body.

Bad Girl

The days that were spent
like breakable money
saved inside me
as I saved myself for some deeper experience.

The nights that were long,
unending,
as the cravings were just beginning.
I was so afraid of sinning.

Now I have sinned
in many new ways,
like when I ate myself blue,
when food was all I had.

There was my own private space
where nobody could enter.
When I wanted to die,
food became my center.

Now I have felt real pleasure
as a wild woman—
a bad girl—
like when I hid those midnight snacks
between the cracks.

Now I have allowed myself to scream,
to dream
of danger,
of being naked under my own sunlight.

Food was the fire
for this devilish pyromaniac;
all the matches were lit
in my own child's playground.

I was a bad girl
where nobody could hear,
nobody could see,
the hungry person inside of me.

Lost in greasy creations
with only food as my guide.
Was there a monster
waiting eagerly inside?

Now I know there is no monster,
only a woman,
imperfect—
unlike food.

When the Lights Dim

At dinner she sits so quietly,
barely touches her meal.
She is unable to tell him her feelings,
she is so afraid to feel.

He talks about his job,
his latest business proposal,
while she listens from the kitchen,
emptying her food into the garbage disposal.

In bed he holds her close,
can never quite reach
that secret place in her mind
where she is feeling unworthy
like a child left behind.

She waits for the click of the light switch,
the silence of the night,
the sound of his snoring,
and the hunger pains she's been ignoring.

She sneaks out of bed,
hoping the stairs won't creak
as she rushes down,
feeling hungry and weak.

It's always there waiting:
chips,
cookies,
bread;
all the words that haven't been said.

She can't tell him she hurts,
that sometimes she's ready to scream.
Chocolate sauce muffles her sounds;
ice cream becomes her lost dream.

She takes it in with gusto;
faster and faster she stuffs,
cold leftover pizza,
a pint of Häagen Dazs.
She doesn't even stop and pause.

It seems to go on forever,
yet it's over in the blink of an eye,
when she finally has to ask herself,
why?

Why does she make herself suffer
alone at 1 a.m. on the kitchen floor?
Why does she keep needing more and more?

Why does she fill up so completely
without really enjoying the taste?
Wanting to throw up,
is she bulimic
or just overstuffed?

Why can't she tell her mother,
her husband,
her boss,
that they make it hard
for her to let down her guard?

So she lets it down with food.
Her food has seen her in every mood.
For just a moment she feels safe
until it is over
and then she feels sick.

She feels like she is the one in control,
letting food be the only way to her soul—
a soul that is hungry for so much more.

Wilma's Potato Saga

It lies in front of me, lines of age throughout its hard oval-shaped existence. It has a face that depicts the ugliness of hopeless distress and anger. It has a small hole at its bottom, seeming to suck in the dryness of my mood, for this potato becomes more gruesome by the second.

I think of the Indians and how they huddle together by a campfire somewhere in New Mexico. The ground on which they sit is as brown as my potato, brown as their rapidly wrinkling skin, brown as a memory crying to be relived.

I shall continue to examine my potato, knowing with pain in my heart that it was once nature's potato and in truth always will be. Nonetheless, it is mashed, fried and chewed harshly between hungry teeth. Even I shall strip it until it is humiliated by its nakedness. It will then be in my stomach, quickly digested.

I am now caressing my potato, ashamed of myself for feeling such desperate hunger for it. I touch it so gently, but even if it should feel tickled, I know it will not bear a smile. How can a human being such as I destroy such ugly beauty? How can I think so little of its desire to live, possibly to marry a fellow potato someday? Who do I think I am anyway?

It is solved! My problem is no more! I shall bow my head toward its unspeakable malice and be punished by the God of potatoes! Hit me, darn potato! One of us has to go!

Personal Reflections

Photo: Jeff Handler

1990—165 pounds.

Hungry and Helpless

Having diabetes always made me feel different and set apart from the other kids. I grew up feeling embarrassed by all my special dietary needs; I was denied foods that other kids could have freely.

Every day was an up-and-down roller-coaster ride. I felt so out of control, as if my blood sugars were controlling me. In a sense, they were.

My father liked to move a lot, so I never really felt settled. Up until he died in 1994, we had moved eight times. When I was ten and he moved us from California to New York City, it seemed like a hurricane was taking everything I knew away.

Again, I felt out of control. I felt scared and unsettled. I had some learning disabilities and emotional problems, as did most of the kids in my new school. I began acting out my rage and helplessness. So with my diabetes, problems at school, and puberty soon approaching, I was one angry and confused child.

In addition, the two different teachers that my class had to endure that year were enough to send anyone into hysterics. They each handled things too harshly, and I believe they were let go partially for that reason. They seemed to get pleasure out of showing how authoritative they were, and the kids had no control over being physically dragged out of the room if they misbehaved.

When things got too much for me to handle, I would break into song, and it didn't matter if I was disrupting a class or not. My hidden voice was coming out and I was going to be heard. I was highly knowledgeable about music and could sing many songs that kids my age wouldn't usually know.

The teachers eventually put my desk out in the hall. Sometimes they even covered my mouth with their chalky hands, and that made me feel even more helpless.

Eventually, I met a teacher who recognized my talents and saw that I was just desperately trying to express myself. She became my teacher for the next two years and helped me to discover my writing talent, and helped the other kids to express themselves through acting improvisation. I began to feel more in control as I took singing lessons and wrote poetry.

It wasn't until I turned thirteen that my problems with food started. I suddenly realized I was out of that school where they had restricted my food and soda intake. Junior high school was due to start in a few months and I knew that nobody would care about what I ate.

That summer, I began changing physically. I had gotten my first period and was filling out. Unfortunately, I chose the wrong place to spend my summer—I spent it in California with my grandparents, at their Malibu beach house.

According to my grandmother, I needed to lose weight. I had never thought of myself as fat and, for the first time in my life, I was beginning to wonder. I wasn't fat, I was filling out. I wasn't a stick, but that hadn't bothered me before. I felt normal and okay, that is, until I had to listen to my grandmother tell me that I wasn't.

Going shopping with my grandmother was emotionally

painful. I couldn't fit into those small Malibu sizes and I was the one who had to change, rather than the clothes. I had to fit the size. From that point on, I became more and more obsessed with fitting the size and the more obsessed I became, the more I ate.

Food became my place where I could hide and be alone. I would eat separately from the family and watch television. It was as if food understood all my rage and that stuffing my face was a form of expression that I couldn't share with anyone.

That summer greatly affected the image I had of myself. I believe that my grandmother was always concerned about my well-being where my diabetes was concerned. But she never really understood the disease and I was always trying to explain it to her. She just didn't trust me to take care of myself, and that would frustrate me and cause me to spite her by overeating in front of her.

When I say she didn't understand the disease, I mean that she didn't understand carbohydrates. For example, she would forbid me to put syrup on my French toast, but then would turn around and offer me a glass of orange juice, which has just as much carbohydrate as syrup does. The arguments we would have ended up elevating my blood sugar even more than the syrup would have, so she ended up defeating her own goal of keeping my blood sugars down by causing me to feel so helpless and argumentative.

I had very dangerous blood sugar levels that summer, and every time I go to California, I still have them. I see California as the place where the word "FAT" first became an issue for me. Malibu can be a very superficial place and I've had to come to accept the fact that I will never have that perfect Malibu body. The injections I have taken over the years have also made that impossible.

Insulin causes fat cells to stick to the diabetic like glue. Then there is the matter of scar tissue and excess skin that the injections themselves cause. My stomach is so destroyed by scar tissue that I can barely feel the muscles underneath. I have been receiving injections every day since I was three and now that I am older, I take about four to five injections a day.

I always admire the thin diabetic but I know that, for me, diabetes has definitely gotten in the way of my successfully controlling my hunger and my weight. I have been on one fad diet after another, and all that diets have led to is a further time-consuming obsession.

All that this obsession leads to is pain. I don't fit the size. I never will. I have made myself sick trying to have that perfect Malibu body. I have a beautiful body and I even have a nice curvaceous figure, but I am not thin. I am a sexy, full-figured woman of substance, and the size will just have to expand to fit me.

Barbie, My Flawless Sister

Barbie has always been like a flawless sister to me. Between us there has been a rivalry, silent and eternal. It was a rivalry I could not confront because she is made of plastic. We fought for grandma's attention. Whenever grandma came to New York to visit our family, there was Barbie, gleaming like a perfect diamond somewhere in the background. Usually, grandma would visit New York to fulfill some sort of business for Mattel. There was usually some function involving Toy Show or some honor that she was due to receive.

That is not to say that she didn't want to see us. I know that she loves us and that Barbie was not nearly as important as her family; but then again, Barbie also is her family. At times, grandpa would defend Barbie as if she were one of his children. "She is a doll. A sweet, lovable doll." He spoke of her as if she were so precious, that nobody would dare say otherwise in front of him.

Well, it is difficult to compete with something that perfect. Barbie could do no wrong. For me, on the other hand, the inadequacies were endless. I always needed to lose weight, I hated school, I didn't have normal good health, I would never finish what I started and most of all, I was this huge mass of imperfection compared to my flawless sister, Barbie. Of course, I now realize that I am a living, breathing human being, therefore imperfect.

Barbie could be anything she wanted. By the time puberty hit me in the face, Barbie had started and completed more careers than any woman could ever dream possible. I was lost. I didn't know who I was, but I always felt left out somehow.

I felt left out of the spotlight. Barbie had the spotlight and I felt as though I was fading into some secret cage where I couldn't get out. I had a great singing voice, but unlike Barbie, I had to work at it. If Barbie wanted to become a famous singer, all Mattel had to do was put a microphone in her hand and dress her up the right way. Barbie had it all, but as I grew up, I began realizing that she didn't have a voice and that she didn't have a say in how she wanted to dress, or anything for that matter.

I realized that I had choices, including how I felt about myself. How a woman feels about herself is much more important than how anybody else feels, and it has taken me years to learn that lesson.

Wrapped in Golden Paper

She came to me wrapped in golden paper
when I was just a child.
"Play with her;
she can be anything you want," I was told.
I could even have her body and fit the mold.

If I worked real hard,
cut out all the fat,
I could be teeny,
dress like her;
even wear a bikini.

She came to me when I was a teen,
looking so perfect
like from a magazine.

She had it all,
a market success;
she became every little girl's dream,
the perfect blonde princess.

She stood out in the toy store aisles
apart from all the rest,
so many young girls' self-esteem
would be put to the test.

The perfect body image for society!
There went the tolerance for variety,
and the quest for perfection continued
with triple the anxiety.

She came to me one Christmas,
wrapped in a special bow.
I untied her,
set her free,
as I remained forever in her captivity.

Sounds of Society

Ruth and Elliot Handler survey their
Barbie and Ken dolls, 1959.

Barbie is, in fact, just a doll, created by one woman and then endorsed time and time again by a society that has spent billions and billions of dollars trying to become the very perfection she radiates. Plastic surgery, diets, and self-starvation are just a few of the many ways women have attempted to have that perfect body. More often than not it results in failure, and leaves women feeling even worse about their bodies. So while society is trying to shape up in the gym to become healthier, what we really have is an unhealthy society, prone to cruelty and disapproval of the less-fit. We are trying so hard to discard anything larger than a size ten from our closets that we are not really living. We are dying inside.

It's unfortunate that Barbie's message hasn't changed much over the years, especially when you consider all the problems associated with body image and how they have affected women everywhere. Her image of perfection has remained and so has the truth of the real human body, and how unattainable Barbie's figure really is. So although she is not entirely to blame, she certainly hasn't helped this downward spiral we find ourselves in today as women.

CELERY
STICKS

Fat Is Funky

Fat is funky,
different,
a change from what is expected.
I guess that is why it is rejected.

Fat is the outcast
locked in its own separate box
in separate clothing stores,
where the material covers what
shouldn't be seen.

Fat is always on the friend
that hangs around the thin girls
who know that fat is no competition
and doesn't have a chance of outshining them.

Fat is stubborn,
can never take a hint;
it is the unwanted chaperone,
the dependent authority figure that demands
attention.

Fat is the annoyance
that surgeons suck away.
The models try to be perfect
as the computers chop away their extras.

Fat is fucked,
and shit out of luck.

Acceptance is disappearing more and more;
bodies are becoming less and less
in a society where less is considered best;
where fat remains funky,
a punishment for the food junkie.

Chaos and Fat-Free Kugel

My mother has always made noodle kugel over the holidays. It was always my father's and my favorite dish. After I got married, suddenly my life and my family's life were spent at my in-laws' dinner table.

My mother-in-law made fat-free kugel for the holidays and blatantly rejected my mother's offer to make hers, which was made the real way. I'll never forget how I felt: new family, new life, and fat-free kugel. I remember how my mother-in-law announced all the fat-free foods before putting them on the table.

A year later, she made another kugel in its true fattening form, and I was hurt and angry that she could have made it the real way, yet had refused my mother's a year earlier.

My father had passed away months earlier and it was very important to me to have that kugel, and to have something to hold onto other than the new life that my in-laws were always trying to force on me. It is amazing how something that small can turn into such a monster inside you and, before you know it, you have eaten enough for twenty monsters. Instead of talking about it to my mother-in-law, I let it build up for two years before I was able to let it go. Silence in a fat-free society will surely make you fat, if it doesn't kill you first.

Come eat at my place
I promise to get right in your face

Dinner at Deidre's
(Echoes of a Meddlesome Mother-in-Law)

If anyone can take the danger out of a dessert,
it is I;
I promise it won't hurt.

If slimness shall be won,
if taste shall be none,
come eat at my place;
I promise to get right in your face.

I will tell you what is healthy,
what is sin.
If the monotony doesn't kill you,
it will at least make you thin.

I'll tell you about veggies,
about every substitute in the book.
Your taste buds will adjust;
there's no getting off the hook.

In a world that replaces
what has been enjoyed by the tongue,
there is no room for mistakes—
only lots of exercise and fat-free cakes.

Come try my recipes,
my advice,
my lifestyle;
join me in my rightful place in society;
become a stereotype for awhile.

Sushi never tasted so good, 1993.

I think it's very interesting about men and women in today's world of dating and personal ads. I find it funny when I call the voice personals and a man complains that he can't find the love he's looking for.

He wants love, compassion, and sensitivity from a woman. But she must be thin, fit, successful, and whatever other, limiting qualities he chooses to place on his perfect woman. Women do it, too. We are not so all-accepting either.

It is true that chemistry is important, but does that mean that, if we are not instantly physically attracted to somebody, the feelings won't be there by the third or fourth date? And if we want more than just to get laid, doesn't it make sense that we should look for more than just the physical? The physical can change, so never fall in love with the physical. It may disappoint you, as the real person underneath may, once the stars and fireworks disappear.

Unfortunately, a lot of us don't wait around for even the first date with somebody different from our so-called type. We reject so many wonderful people for this fantasy ideal of perfection we have, and then wonder why love has passed us by.

Johnny's Declaration

I am writing this ad in search of love.
You must be a beauty
dropped from the sky above.

You must have long hair,
be of normal size and weight;
if not, with me you will never get a date.

Please be socially acceptable,
accomplished and employed.
Please look good in tight clothes;
too much bulge gets me annoyed.

Please wear no more than a size ten dress,
be no more than 130 pounds.
I am looking for a goddess,
one who astounds.

I am extremely open-minded,
love lots of things,
love most music—
except when the fat lady sings.

You can have eyes like an angel,
a heart of gold,
but if your body doesn't match,
with me you won't grow old.

I don't like games,
so only serious women need reply,
and if you don't
I will understand why.

Pretty Cruelty

Here it is;
a world of pretty bodies.
Just look at all the soap operas,
shampoo commercials,
makeup advertisements!

It is true,
fat isn't pretty.
Cruelty is uglier,
but somehow makes the covers of magazines
pretty cruelty at its best.

Plump may not be the most pretty,
but pretty does not a world make.
Bones are mere existing density
where plump puts personality.
Plump is a part of today's reality.

Thin is in,
in a world of ever growing plumpness.
Pretty cruelty has almost won;
Rubens' paintings are cracked
along with the image of the classic woman.

It Is Not Up to the Thin

Thin people have been complaining,
writing in to magazines,
saying that there isn't enough room,
that fat people take up too much space.

Fat people should sit somewhere else
or buy an extra seat,
that being thin gives exclusive rights
to ignorant and petty cruelty.

There is more than enough room
for every type of mankind.
This world was a gift to us;
we have no right to lock anyone out.

If it takes a thin person longer to move
because someone heavier occupies some space,
then that is just too bad—
the thin will have to wait.

The thin will have to manage
in a world that belongs to everybody
and one day,
the thin may become crippled.

What will happen then,
when a thin person might need extra time,
extra space,
and might even draw some attention to themselves?

It is not for the thin to assume
that good looks and mobility will last forever.
It is not up to the thin
to complain about someone else's eating habits.

It is not up to the thin
to deny heavier people jobs,
to make weak excuses
as to why they cannot work like everyone else.

It is not up to the thin
to make fun of and tease
those whom they consider less attractive,
to be harsh and unbending to those who are different.

It is, however, up to all of us
to be decent to one another,
to help each other,
to give each other support.

It is up to the thin not to take for granted
the bodies that they have,
to realize
that one day they might not have them anymore.

RESTAURANT

It's So Easy

It's so easy
to tell me to eat less,
cut out the fat,
shrink my portions in half.

It's easy for someone who can't see
or even begin to feel
the pain of a problem
that for many has become so real.

Giving up the food I love
is not an option.
Being fat isn't either.
I guess I'm stuck.

There's nowhere to go
when stuck in between
reality
and a fashion magazine.

Isn't it getting old
being counseled,
being told,
how to modify perfectly human desires,

how to appear for society,
the proper look and figure,
how it is unattractive
to be bigger?

It is not so easy
being bigger
in a shrinking society
where fat is the enemy soldier.

Dangerous Delusions

I am not bulimic, anorexic, or obese, but I have suffered for so long with a body-image disorder that I have considered each of those options at desperate times. I am a thirty-year-old woman. I have lived my life battling the bulge and now that I have grown up and matured into the person that food has kept me from finding, it is not only scary, but difficult to comprehend sometimes.

The Outstretched Mirror

The shower steam fogs my view,
thank God!
Now I won't have to see the blob.

Soon I know the fog will dissipate
and the outstretched mirror will reveal
the ugliness of me,
my own warped reality.

The mirror stretches
as if it were being pulled by my conscience
by all the horrible things I ate yesterday.

Just yesterday I looked like myself;
now I don't know this person in the mirror.
Who is she
and why is she so fat?

My clothes feel tight,
when just yesterday they seemed to fit.
How can it be,
that I gained so much weight in one night?

How can I look good in one mirror
and so fat in another?
Is this my mind playing tricks,
or are these really my hips?

My hips looked normal last night;
now they are wide.
Is this outstretched mirror the reason
why I feel so fat inside?

The mirror stretches every way
every day.
I just get bigger and bigger.
I stretch forever
in a mirror that forever stretches the truth.

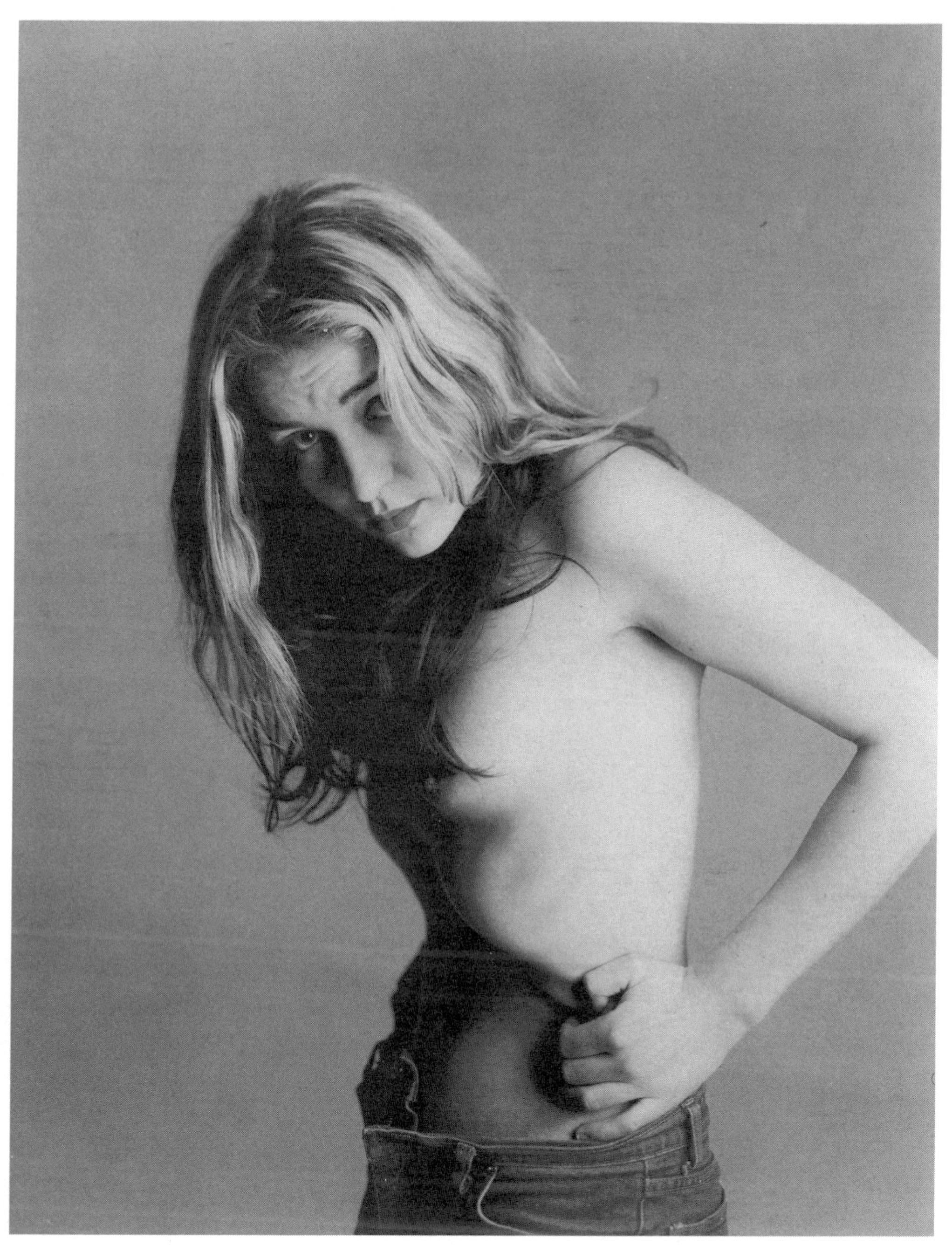

Photo: Julie Meinich Jacobesen

Elliot Handler

Bones

Lost in this world of bones,
mine are finally showing.
Once upon a time they were hidden
under the fat that was forbidden.

Now it's all gone,
the cellulite,
the flab.
Now there is nothing more of me to grab.

People want me to come back
from the hell of starvation.
I don't know what they mean;
it's just diet dedication.

A grapefruit a day,
the rest shoved under the bed.
People say
I'm already dead.

See my new body,
a totally new me!
A skeleton I'm not;
that's just their fantasy.

Lost in this world of bones
where nobody can see,
the decay comes from inside
this humble slave to vanity.

Secret Stashes

Linda hides her chocolate behind the mantel,
hoping once again she won't get caught,
her body suffering the merciless attack
of cruel fat onslaught.

Katie sneaks out of her bed at night,
looking for more to purge—
rummages through her roommate's snack drawer,
finds lots of goodies to fill the urge.

Wendy tells her parents she'll eat in her room;
leaving all her meal unfinished,
she hides her portion under her bed
so as not to reveal why her body has diminished.

Marcy has her secret place
for diet pills, cigarettes,
anything to stop the craving;
food was her secret way of misbehaving.

Edith and her friends had too much to eat,
threw up, got home in a bad mood,
told her mother they were drunk
because anything was better than too much food.

Carol orders only a salad and dry fish
at most family dinners,
only to get home, pick up the phone,
becoming the queen of take-out sinners.

Lisa hid her M&Ms from her critical husband.
Their trust once had no bounds
until he dug a hole for her secrets;
burying her under her added pounds.

Around the world,
across the nation,
all of this secret activity
causing such a destructive sensation.

One woman dresses in black,
batting her dark mascara lashes,
while another joins in the parade
of painful secret stashes.

Food Magician

I am the food magician.
Look at it gleaming on my plate!
Into my tummy it goes;
where it ends up,
nobody but me knows.

Such thrilling conversation
at each long, drawn-out meal!
Nobody can even begin to sense
the pain that I feel
when my magic wand is waved.

Out from my magic hat
a rose,
a rabbit—
what started out as magic
has now become a bad habit.

So many tricks!
The food just disappears
unlike the memories
of painful pressured years.

So much food
passing through my lips.
Poof!
Down the toilet;
it never sees my hips.

People ask me, what's my trick?
I laugh,
crying inside as I choke on a bread stick,
barely making it down a throat so sore
into a body that is sick,
that will soon be no more.

I Wish I Looked Just Like You

I wish I looked just like you,
so perfect and pretty,
new and shiny from the toy store.
You can be a doctor, a stewardess;
everything and so much more.

You look like someone I know,
like from that magazine,
that lady with the swimsuit—
my brother has her on his wall;
he says she's really cute.

He says girls like that are perfect.
Mommy says if I eat too much
I'll never look like that,
like when I had that ice cream
for an afternoon snack.

My friend Donna says,
if I want to look just like you,
I'll have to eat all my food like a good little girl:
Sneak into the bathroom,
throw it up when I'm through.

My sister gets teased at school.
Mommy says she is fat.
It makes me sad.
I'd rather die
than look like that.

Tell me how to have your body?
That's my dream for when I grow up,
to be just like you.
I'll do anything,
even throw it up when I'm through.

Photo: Ken Handler

Personal Reflection

High on Ketosis

Ketosis is a state that a person goes into when they are on an extremely low carbohydrate diet. Since I am not a medical doctor, I cannot make a medical statement that ketosis is an eating disorder. I can however, explain how ketosis affected me and what I went through.

For me, ketosis became an eating disorder. I went into ketosis as my marriage was coming to an end. I cut out all carbohydrates and ate all the bacon, eggs, cream, butter and red meat that I wanted to. It was like heaven. I felt such power sitting at the table eating all the good stuff, while other people had to eat dry fish and small portions in order to maintain their diet.

I felt untouchable, like nobody could hurt me anymore. My feelings were masked by the ketosis. I felt like I was on a drug. At times, I was overly hyper, and other times I couldn't even get out of bed. My breath was disgusting and frequently, so was my mood. Ketosis was my joy ride that wound and turned in so many directions, some of them quite destructive.

I ended up in the hospital with a kidney stone and my cholesterol went up to 474. I suffered from short-term memory loss. Sometimes I couldn't even finish my sentences. The eating disorder became evident when I wouldn't stop. Thin was more important than my kidneys, more important than my diabetes, more important than life. Fat became an image of death for me. Even when I dropped thirty pounds, I still felt fat. It was not enough. I would have died trying to find that place they call, "enough." I struggled daily, thinking about my body at least twelve hours a day. Every mirror I passed became my worst enemy. There were days I wanted to die.

Ketosis continued floating around my crazy atmosphere, as if it were a balloon, promising to pop. Truthfully, I find myself still on a ketonic diet. After I overcame my first bout with ketosis, I tried the low-fat approach to weight loss. My body rebelled against the carbohydrates and I put on twenty pounds in a very short time.

In my experience, ketosis became addictive and my body became unresponsive to any diet that involved more than one carbohydrate meal a day. One carbohydrate meal has worked beautifully for me in terms of maintaining my weight and even losing a little bit. But ketosis still remains on the sidelines, waiting for me to return to it. It is like the abusive relationship that you want and need to abandon, but end up returning to out of fear or desperation.

A few weeks ago, my dog died right in front of me. My child was gone and I felt totally helpless and out of control. A week later, I was back in ketosis. I was very sad, and I was crying all the time. My eating became so out of control that I needed the ketosis to put me in line. Ketosis is a natural appetite suppressant and makes me unable to eat a lot.

I am not happy about being back in ketosis, especially because of my diabetes. A diabetic goes into ketosis anyway, when his/her blood sugar is out of control. A ketonic diet just adds further complications to a diabetic's already complicated existence; at least, that is what my doctor has told me. In my opinion, ketosis can be abused like anything else, and I have abused it at times when my life gets to be too much for me to handle.

I have abused myself by not drinking enough water, which is essential to flush out the ketones and the kidneys. The dehydration feels terrible, but as I feel my rib cage beginning to show again, I really don't care. Sometimes, I just sleep it off and wake up with a dry mouth. I deprive myself of all carbohydrates, and watch as my body changes in the mirror.

It isn't so much that I want to get thin. It's that I want to control something in my life. I want my dog back. I miss my father. Relationships and sex become hard to control. Carbohydrates become hard to control. I become terrified of the complete and total loss of control and of myself, so ketosis seems like something that will snap me back.

In my opinion, ketosis did hurt me. It tricked me into feeling like I was powerful, while all the time, I was under its control. I have heard that eating disorders are like that. I am just telling it like it is—or I should say, how I have known it to be. Eating disorders are very confusing and painful, no matter which form they take.

Maybe ketosis itself is not an eating disorder. But for me, being in it over a long period of time, it became just like one. I know there are a few select doctors out there who endorse and highly recommend the ketonic diet as a safe form of weight loss. I also know that a bigger percentage of doctors are against ketosis, and this argument has gone on for a long time. I think that doctors who endorse ketosis should be aware of somebody like me, somebody who developed a disorder from what they consider to be a healthy and safe diet.

I don't think enough people understand how vulnerable a woman can be to a potential eating disorder. The physical aspects of a person are not all that should be accounted for. What about a person's mental state? A woman goes on a diet, thinking she will become thin, but she also can think that her whole life will be better and she can end up extremely empty and disappointed. I thought I was the queen of the universe when I was in ketosis. It started out as a diet and ended up my own personal power crusade.

I didn't feel so powerful as I undressed to get into my hospital gown. I didn't feel so powerful being examined in a noisy, crowded emergency room. I was in terrible pain. The doctors knew it was a kidney stone. I flirted with this one doctor because I felt so sad and flirting was the only way I knew how to make myself feel good. He thought I was attractive and I remember his attention being so important to me at the time. I still wanted to be the ketosis queen.

Even after all the following days, when they injected me with pain killers and pumped me up with so much water that I couldn't fit into anything for weeks—even then, I wanted to stay in ketosis. I wanted my power back.

I am still struggling with ketosis, but am much more focused and aware of the dangers and the precautions I need to take. I will probably go back to the one carbohydrate meal a day as soon as I can. I know that I have power, with or without ketosis. This book has brought an enormous sense of control and well-being to my life. I hope that I can continue using my words as a positive source of power, with the hope that maybe women can recognize their own power even when in the grip of an eating disorder.

Elliot Handler

The Scale Jail

Elliot Handler

Just Ten More Pounds

If I lose just ten more pounds,
my life would be so much better.
135 pounds is too much to weigh;
just ten more pounds
would make this pain go away.

125,
still can't wear these jeans.
My boyfriend hasn't told me he loves me;
I don't love me.

118,
these jeans finally fit.
Tommy broke up with me;
maybe he thought I was too fat.

110,
still don't have a boyfriend.
My parents still barely notice me;
maybe I am disappearing.

98,
I finally got a date
with the family doctor.
Now they notice me!

88 pounds,
going down, down, down.
Now they say they love me,
now that I am completely lost
with a body that can't be found.

The Scale

Help!
I can't get away;
it's coming to get me!

It's alive,
taking complete control—
taking over my mind,
my body,
my soul!

I hide behind bushes,
behind mountains and trees.
Will I ever escape
this frightening social disease?

Sometimes it makes me smile,
tells me nice things;
other times it makes me cry,
laughing as it stings.

Sometimes it keeps me awake
inside my worst nightmare,
makes me see things in the mirror
that aren't really there.

It chases me through my own horror,
through a space with no room.
I squeeze in sheepishly,
sneezing from smoldering perfume,

through clothing store aisles—
sales women with their noses in the air—
through long dressing room battles,
through Barbie's long flowing hair.

I awake screaming,
screaming awake
when I realize
I am not dreaming.

It will tip,
tilt,
fill me with guilt
for the rest of my life.

Locked in jail,
forever the victim
of the scale.

Fear is deeper than body fat.
It is inside the very core of a person,
and that is something that needs to be faced
no matter what the numbers are on the scale.

Steven Cavallo

The Fading Gymnast

I am not sure how much longer I can go on.
I am no longer the perfect athlete;
I am not that strong.
I am so young;
why do I feel so old?

Why am I fading away
like the body I once had
before I was told to lose eight pounds,
that being imperfect was bad?

I lost eight pounds,
and so much more,
just to please you
so you wouldn't show me the door.

Can't you see my agony,
hear my hungry words,
my inner cries,
the part of me that dies
whenever you criticize?

You are my mentor,
my ticket to success,
the perfect coach;
you just want me to be my best.
I don't know if I believe that anymore.

Should I believe in you
when you push and push
until I can't eat,
can't stop purging,
can't land on my feet?

Every move becomes an eternity;
every second becomes hours,
days and days on the bar,
as I flip just for you;
I'm your perfect little star.

My parents don't know me anymore;
I am hidden to them.
They know something is dark inside,
that it is not only my food that I hide,
that the old me has died.

I am no longer a person,
no longer me.
I am simply the trophy
every young athlete's fantasy,

the agile body that gets the applause,
the fading gymnast
who has lost her cause.

Keep Pumping

Time passes me by;
my friends are waiting.
I must keep pumping,
jogging,
lifting and jumping.

Time disappears like cotton candy under a tongue;
all candy will disappear from my thighs.
I will stay forever young
as long as I exercise.

I was 150 pounds last week;
now I'm down almost half a pound.
I am running myself
into the ground.

I work out in the morning,
in the afternoon,
before I go to sleep.
A body like mine
is so hard to keep.

There is no more time for fun,
for romance,
for sex;
there is only time for Cybex.

Cybex is only one of my many machines.
It helps me stay focused;
it keeps my hips in my jeans.

My boyfriend says I'm beautiful,
that I don't need to lose weight,
that I can eat more
than lettuce on a plate.

I don't hear him
or my parents
or my friends,
when they shout
that I over work out.

One hundred sit-ups is never enough
so I do two hundred every day,
anything to make this weight go away.

People think I’m obsessed.
I just want to look my best,
not have time to feel depressed.

Now I’m down a complete size!
There is no better cure for what ails
than exercise.

The Roller Coaster

Got it from an infomercial,
a fashion magazine ad.
My recent experiment
is part of the latest fad.

Grapefruit pills,
starvation,
liquid diets
are taking over the nation.

Don't forget the doctors
sending their clippings in the mail;
they promise you magic pills,
a potion that will never fail.

Read between the lines
on the pages that make you believe
that you can get thin
and still eat with total sin.

Cleanse out your system
with the cabbage soup diet.
Let it all out the back end,
splurge till you drop,
begin again with Fen-phen.

You can try to resist the urge
or when all else fails,
splurge and purge.
That new dress will surely fit tomorrow.

You can always try hypnosis
or bounce around all day,
high on ketosis,
and hope your bad breath goes away.

There's always herbal wraps,
the famous pill called Redux,
or the perfect solution:
a few nips and tucks.

There are so many possibilities:
protein drinks, rice;
on this roller coaster ride
it's so hard to be nice.

It's quite the thrill
living pound by pound.
The scale goes up;
we go down.

It's a constant fun house,
every dark room a different mood,
as we forever fight our war
with food.

Me in 1988—Breakfast was never so enjoyable.

Personal Reflections

A Breath of Fresh Ketosis

I was having dinner with my mother, my sister, and her boyfriend. We were perusing our menus when suddenly there was this horrible, foul odor. My sister wanted to switch chairs with her boyfriend because the smell was making her nauseated. Her boyfriend said it was even worse where he was sitting. He said it smelled as if a skunk had somehow gotten into the room.

We called the waiter over, to ask him to find out what that horrible stench was. The restaurant was full, so we couldn't simply switch tables. It was terrible. The only thing was, I didn't smell it. I had no idea what they were talking about.

About fifteen minutes had gone by when my mother looked over at me and then glanced at my sister.

"No way!" my sister yelled.

It turned out that the horrible, foul odor that had almost ruined everyone's dinner was my very own ketosis breath. "Sorry, guys," I apologized, but was too high on ketosis to pay the situation much attention.

"Is that really coming from you?" my sister asked.

"I'm afraid so," I answered.

We all laughed, especially when the waiter came back to tell us he was unable to pinpoint the source of the odor—or should I say, the unmistakable breath of fresh ketosis.

Used in a Brand-New Body

When I was thin and on one of the biggest ketosis highs of my life, I believed life was perfect. I could have any man I wanted. I went on date after date, and felt sexy and alive for the first time since my marriage.

During my sexual discoveries, I went back to California. I hooked up with two male friends that I hadn't seen in eighteen years. Durk wanted to see my hotel room and although he tried to get me as tipsy as he could, I resisted.

Then there was Pete, for whom I had had special feelings ever since we were kids. Seeing him again was painful. He had lost himself to Scientology and was dead to me forever. I had been starving myself of all nutrients that week; I was eating mainly chicken broth. Somehow my dangerously high ketone level made the pain of losing a childhood friend easier.

I continued to let my ketones take over until I burned off ten pounds in one week. Then I fell for my much older, drug-addicted cousin and, needless to say, disaster was not far behind. I was available and just-about divorced. The ketosis was keeping me numb inside, yet making me appear very sensual on the outside.

Months went by. After I had followed my drug-addicted cousin to Denver—only to have him reject and humiliate me—I knew it was time to move on to greener pastures.

So I started to date the more traditional way. I met new people on a dating phone personals line. I met Jon, who told me he thought I was cute but he believed that his roommate Doug and I would hit it off much better.

Doug was a Texan and very cute. We were instantly attracted to each other. I felt so sexy and thin being out with him. We laughed over Chinese food and then went straight up to my apartment for a glass of Chinese plum wine.

It was the best sex I had ever had. It was wild, uninhibited, and exciting. I was finally letting out all the pent-up tension that my marriage had caused. I remember crying during the sex because I felt so alive. It was like when your hand falls asleep, and then suddenly the feeling comes back like pins and needles. Only, this was my soul that had been asleep, my very being.

I knew that this wasn't the love of my life, but I wanted to continue dating him. I was just not prepared for what happened next.

I really thought being thin would bring me everything. I thought that it was great, attracting men who never would have looked at me before. Well, not only did Doug tell all his friends that I was available for a good time, but one of them even called me up and made sexual advances toward me. He was rude and obnoxious. He tried everything he could to get me to let him up to my apartment.

He said he had followed Doug and me, and watched us eat dinner. He wanted to know if we too, could have a good time? I felt so dirty and invaded. I wanted to become so unattractive and fat that nobody would ever see me as a sex object again.

Being thin only helped me to attract the wrong kind of men. I was attracting the kind of person who was shallow and narrow-minded—everything that I really didn't want in a partner.

I used my body to attract men and my soul became hidden from their view. I believe that Doug saw my soul, but he just couldn't handle more than my skin-deep curves and crevices. The lesson here is, be careful what you wish for. You just might get it, only to realize that it wasn't what you really wanted at all.

Sudden Awakening

I have learned so much about myself since I first began writing this book three years ago. I have recently become more in touch with why I feel the need to control things so much, therefore leading myself down the road of a never-ending battle with food and body image.

It all started when I was three years old and suddenly I found myself in the hospital. I remember seeing the bars of my crib and feeling so contained in a small restricting space.

I remember the echo of my tears as I was stuck by needles, being relieved of blood from my thin, so-small body. I remember doctors hovering over me. Diabetes had invaded my life. It has continued wreaking its havoc on me to this very day, 27 years later.

I was a sensitive child. Diabetes made me feel strange and out of control. It was quite the experience, suddenly waking up in the middle of my classroom with orange juice being forced on me.

At times I felt like I was hallucinating. I would experience perception changes, due to changes in blood sugar. Sometimes I would shake and get scared, thinking or believing that a plant might be looking at me funny. So many things had eyes and just plain looked wacky.

Even though I know that my diabetes played a major role in my strange perceptions, I believe that there were other factors as well. I have come to realize, as an adult, that I am a bit more intuitive than the average person.

For years I worked with people, telling them what I saw and felt. They would want to know when they would be in love, when their job situation would change and other things of personal concern to them.

I will not label myself clairvoyant, or any other name that has tried to be an adjective for these most unusual abilities. I just know that when I foresee things, they happen, and that can be scary at any age. I often wonder if, as a child, I didn't feel the burden of my own sensitivity to different energies around me. Being so creative at such a young age, I'm certain, added to my strange feelings.

Freedom has always been very important to me and the diabetes certainly infringed a lot on what could have been a pretty much carefree childhood. I was forced to watch every meal and make sure that I didn't miss it. I had to snack all the time. So, you can see where the food issue first started. Meals were such an every-moment issue for me that I never knew what to do to make eating less important. To this day, I still don't.

There were many factors in my life that caused me to binge, and that determined how I feel about my body. This is as naked as I have ever been on paper. But if it will do some good, if somebody can relate at all to my experiences, then it is time to abandon cover.

I am going to do this in two different parts. The first part is about what, or should I say who, has helped me to open up my feelings again. In the second part, I will go deep inside to a place where it was once very dark and scary. But if I am to strip down to where my body image feelings really began, I need to revisit that place.

PART I

Sudden Awakening

Something remarkable has happened to me over the last few weeks. I have suddenly found myself able to recognize when I am full, therefore being able to cut down my portions. I have come to realize what the food has been covering, and I was able to do that by allowing myself to feel again; feeling again came about through some very enlightening telephone conversations.

I was involved in a very difficult, painful relationship about a year and a half ago. During that time, I disappeared behind a warped mirror where I saw this huge person who couldn't feel anymore. I was overweight, but not nearly as large as the image I perceived. When this relationship ended, I became a member of a phone personals system, where I then connected with a man named Damian. He penetrated into the many different, more complex layers of my being. We spent hours on the phone.

It has always been very important for me to feel in control, to know what I am feeling, to understand it and to analyze it. Then there is this part of me that wants so badly to let go and experience vulnerability. Unfortunately, after my marriage and previous unhappy relationship, I went so deep into hiding that I couldn't come out. But when Damian brought me out, everything came back inside me like pins and needles.

My body image started changing for the better as our phone conversations increased. When I allowed myself to lose control and feel, that is when food suddenly became less important. He brought out more dialogue and honesty in me than I ever thought I could share with another human being. Granted, I am the open and honest type, because otherwise I wouldn't have been able to write this book. But with a complete stranger over the phone, I have never been so forthcoming and vulnerable.

Now let me tell you about how it felt to finally meet this man face to face, this person that I had shared so much with. It was like I was slipping out of control down a waterslide. I was afraid of drowning. I didn't feel the clothes on my body. I felt topless in front of him and I held myself like I felt topless. I came off less self-assured than I had been on the telephone and he pointed that out to me.

I sat there and faced him, teary-eyed as he pointed out every reason why we shouldn't become an item. Of course, every negative I had to counteract with a positive. Suddenly, it occurred to me that I was trying to sell myself to this man. I was boosting myself up like I was meant for him. He had used my body-image problems as one of his reasons why I might not be the right woman for him, and that really hurt me. I became more withdrawn, using shyness as my excuse for not being so vivacious. I was embarrassed by my obvious attempt to alter his opinions. I felt like it was so apparent that I wanted a relationship with him, that I became more analytical myself. We both hid behind our insecurities. I believe that subconsciously he felt naked and analyzed himself, so he needed to take me down a peg. He needed us to be on the same footing. I felt like I was on no footing. His eyes proceeded to remove me from my gravity. At one point I wanted to cry and run away, but I knew that if I did, McDonald's would not be far behind.

We still managed to connect, despite his negativity and my less confident demeanor. As always, I returned to my body image issue, feeling as if maybe he thought I was much fatter than in the picture I had sent him. I guess I felt fat and we now know that when loss of control is evident, fat becomes pretty convenient to hide behind.

It has now occurred to me what I was doing. Instead of telling him how I felt, instead of letting him know that I was hurt and that I needed him to hold me, I hid behind my own negative self-image. I finally opened up to him, letting him know that I felt hurt by what he said. I told him that I felt naked, that I was very emotional and that I needed to feel and that feeling is what being alive means to me.

He then softened, I became less talkative, and our lips found each other's in midtown Manhattan while we were sheltered from a summer downpour.

Another reason why I was so insecure on that rainy afternoon had to do with my power and sexuality. The next section of this book will go deeper into this subject. For now, I will say that with Damian, I was holding back much of my personal power. My lack of confidence partially stemmed from not wanting to show too much, because men have previously fled from my strength. Essentially, I was using my negative body image as a shield to hide my personal power from him.

I guess I was afraid that if I appeared too strong and confident, he would think that I was soliciting some type of physical situation, where I would then be viewed as an easy lay and not as a deep, serious woman who needs and wants to be loved.

I am learning that I don't need to be built up by another human being and that I don't need to try to convince a man that I am worthy, but that is a hard lesson to learn because men tend to throw me off center sometimes. I sometimes need to remind myself that physicality is okay and that for me, it is usually romance and love that I am seeking through a physical union.

Unfortunately, my first experiences with touch of a sexual nature had nothing to do with love, and that brings me to this painful soul-bearing next chapter.

PART II

Childhood Closets

At this moment, I feel a yearning inside that will not go away. Since I am intuitive, highly sensitive and extremely creative, I live my life with intense feelings in my gut. I eat at times just to avoid feeling such intensity. Popcorn at the movies can mask my tears during the emotional scenes, my strong desire to be held, when there is no man beside me in the darkness of the theatre.

Food has done a lot for me, everything except help me to deal with all these feelings. I am pure woman and sensuality. Deep down, I love my body and want to connect to it in many new, exciting ways. I would like to know what it feels like to be in an open field of grass, totally naked. How would my body feel, not caring about anything, but running through the grass and then plopping down in hysterical laughter?

These thoughts bring me to the next part of my self-protection. Sometimes, there is nothing more exciting than the human body and all its vast sensations. When someone is being tickled, it usually renders the body weightless and out of control.

Well, weightless sounds good. The grass caressing my body; a lover running a feather down all my sensitive places. Perhaps at that moment, size would mean nothing. There would be nothing to hide from. Letting myself go would be beautiful and enlightening.

Sometimes when I overeat, I won't let anybody touch me. Tickling becomes out of the question. Now if I do use food so that nobody can touch me, why is that? Well, I was such a ticklish, sensitive child, and with the diabetes and early bouts with food control issues, I was grasping for control. Even approaching age thirty, control remains such an issue for me. I believe that there are some closets where I am still locked in as a little girl, trying to deal with her innocent body and all of its demands and invasions.

The diabetes certainly invaded my young body and demanded so much from it. I wish I could say that diabetes was the only thing that took over my body. My childhood body was so full of feelings and sensations, that I had to eat just to keep them in check.

To this day, I don't remember the exact sequence of events. I do remember the day that Evan, my eighteen-year-old male babysitter, took me to the doctor. My mother had asked him to. He was a friend of the family's, so my parents thought nothing of it. I was eight or nine and we were living in California at the time.

I freaked out at the idea of Evan accompanying me to such a private place. The doctor always touched me on my belly and did normal exams that needed to be done on a child. I didn't want Evan to watch as the doctor looked inside my very private place. I didn't want him to see me take off my clothes and then have to lie naked on the exam table.

Evan, of course, waited in the waiting room, but that didn't matter. I was bothered by the mere fact of his being there. I did my usual fidgeting as the doctor did his exam. I remember lying there, dreading the moment when his hands would go down to the place where I really had no control and where I was very ticklish. Suddenly, as he opened the lips of my vagina to peek inside, the sound of my own laughter triggered an analogy in my young mind.

What the doctor was doing felt exactly like what Evan had done to me. It was just like our crawling finger game that we would sometimes play.

As soon as my parents left for the evening, they would give me instructions to get into my nightgown and get ready for bed. Evan would be waiting for me in my room. He would be seated on a chair, smiling at me, reveling in my feeling uneasy and sheepish. I would lock myself in the bathroom and change into my nightgown, feeling shy and scared to go back into the bedroom.

He always had the bed turned down. Soon we would be under the covers together. His hands and fingers would be all over me. He took off my nightgown and explored every inch of my body. I remember having my back to him and lying on my side.

I didn't understand what he was doing or why. I just knew that I felt weird about it. It was the strangest feeling. It was like playing doctor but then why did I feel so uncomfortable? Those are the questions a child asks when they don't know quite what is happening to them. I will tell you this, control was out the window. He told me that my armpits were sexy and nice and then he teased me about how obviously ticklish I was. I remember trying so hard to stay in control and not laugh or feel anything. He then went to my very private place, the place where I should have had some control, but had it taken away from me.

There was one time when we were in the kitchen together. I looked over at him and saw him staring at me in a way that I didn't understand. I suddenly realized that the nightgown I was wearing was too loose on me and was starting to fall down around my right shoulder. One of my nipples was exposed and he stared at it until I quickly covered myself and ran out of the room. I didn't understand embarrassment at the time, and that my reaction was normal. He made me feel shy, embarrassed and just plain weird.

There were many times where he made me feel powerless. I wanted to tell my parents about what went on with us and he said he would have to deny it and that they wouldn't believe me. It had to remain our little secret.

When my family and I traveled to Europe, Evan came along. Sometimes he would lose his temper. Once when the two of us were alone in our London hotel room, he got mad at me about something and threatened to beat my head in with a pillow. He said that it would be over very quickly and that nobody would blame him. I was frightened, but when I told my parents what he had said, they thought he was just fooling around. So, here was this man who had gently fondled me and now was threatening to hurt me. So gentleness signified guilt and guilt was punished with anger and violence. What a message to receive at nine years old.

Because of what happened with Evan, doctor's exams became unbearable and I became resistant to anyone seeing my body without my consent. I remember having a heat rash at school when all this was going on. My friend Cindy had one too, and we were both asked into the nurse's office. Cindy lifted up her shirt to show the nurse, but I refused. I had the teachers bugging me for hours. To make matters worse, since they couldn't get me to lift my shirt in private, they asked me again in my classroom. I really thought they were stupid, because if I wouldn't lift my shirt in private, why would I do it in front of my class?

They ended up telling my mother, but that did little good. I still wouldn't give in, even when we got home. Finally, my mother threatened no television if I didn't show her my rash. Since I grew up in the seventies and had been a very avid Brady Bunch watcher, I gave in. But I remember how I felt so out of control about something as simple as lifing my shirt.

Years later, I am a nudist at heart, but am still coming into my own sense of self within my body. Because I was made aware at a very young age about how sexy my armpits were, they are now my favorite part of my body. I guess I subconsciously see them as one of the most private hidden places, that when exposed signifies surrender. What happened with Evan was a sick kind of surrender, but there was this part of me that did trust him. He was supposed to take care of me and protect me when my parents were out. I didn't understand why I couldn't tell my parents about out little game. Why did I feel so strange inside, so trapped in a darkness that at times seemed to almost take over my thoughts?

It was horrible, walking around every day feeling like something wasn't quite right. I felt guilty and wanted to talk about it, but didn't know how. I used to hear laughter coming from my parent's bedroom. When I realized that it was a tickling fight between my parents and two younger siblings, I would walk away in disgust. It didn't make sense to me how they could find such joy in tickling each other, and I wanted no part of it. It seemed like too much of an invasion to me, the idea of allowing myself to be tickled and vulnerable.

The only way I knew how to explore my feelings was to masturbate and take off my clothes in front of certain male friends. I know that Evan must have made me touch his penis because my obsession with male genitalia became overwhelming for a while; and then at some point, I didn't want a penis within ten feet of me.

I was made to feel things that I wasn't ready to feel or even comprehend at such a young age. It did add to my sense of aliveness and intensified my already intense mind. Unfortunately, it continued to negatively influence my behavior around boys.

My behavior around one boy in particular became inappropriate. He was a friend from school and I just couldn't keep my hands off him. I had to tickle him. It became an obsession, to the point where I had to stop hanging around him. I would think about him at night and tremble with sexual frustration. I had been introduced to dangerous pleasure. I wanted more, but I wanted to be the one in control. I wanted to do the tickling and decide where and when clothes would be removed.

First of all, intercourse really means very little to me. It is the hugging and kissing and loving that gets my heart palpitating. Even as a child, penises seemed so out of place in my life. Evan used to pee in front of me. Once he even offered to pee on me. I found his genitals disgusting and wanted nothing to do with them. I declined, of course, and he didn't force the issue.

I didn't lose my virginity until I was nineteen. In my opinion, I still could have waited. I felt nothing but the feeling of having to do it. There was no emotion. It was just an act needing to be played out. Sex is a chore when it is not right, and it wasn't the right person for me. He immediately left me to go play basketball, and I was numb, under the covers with a few drops of blood on the sheets.

I've always considered my first love to be Joey, this passionate Latino guy whom I met and fell for right around my sixteenth birthday. Our relationship was short-lived and painful at its end. But I do know what makes me look back on it with such a special fondness. It is the innocence of our physical connection. Joey was the first to introduce me to a touch that wasn't dirty or shameful. We never had intercourse, but I felt more alive than ever in his arms. Sex had nothing to do with any feelings involving my first experiences with love. My body image was great when I was with him. I was quite chunky at the time, but he didn't care. He found me sexy and appealing, as well as intense and emotional. We were both intense and were not afraid to cry together when listening to music and letting ourselves be human within that all-consuming haze of young love.

So now that I have grown up and come into myself through all of this exploration, I think I finally understand much more about the reasons behind a lot of my food and body image issues. I think what I was subconsciously doing with food—by not letting someone tickle or touch me—was protecting myself from dirty feelings. When a child is fondled, it feels very wrong, but it can also feel good. I know that isn't true for a lot of people, but I felt good being touched, even though I was riddled with shame and confusion. Once grown up, I guess I always associated feeling good with some form of guilt. Part of me thrives on it, while another part of me continues to stuff down multiple Big Macs.

The part of me that thrives on the guilt is very sexual and very into exploration. I was taught young that sexual play can be fun, but in my subconscious, there is that glimpse of weirdness that Evan brought to my life.

My food and body-image problems stemmed from intense loss of control. Control of my body, my blood sugars, my vagina, my family's constant relocating, my grandmother's criticism about my diet and weight and in the later years, the death of my father, and finally, a verbally abusive marriage.

It isn't just food that women use to hide behind. It is their own distorted body image. I know that I eat just to avoid intimacy. I also know that just thinking I am fat will achieve the same negative result. Also, I think that feeling fat gives me an excuse not to feel attractive, therefore not letting a man know that I am a sexual being. Not wanting to be viewed as easily "Fuckable," I make myself feel ugly. It is a way of not allowing myself to be hurt. Being molested made me feel very out of control sexually and has probably influenced my choice in partners as well. If a man verbally abuses me or makes me feel bad, I just hide behind a negative body image. Perhaps hiding behind this bad image has worked in the past, but I am ready to experience a beautiful body image, which I can only achieve by not choosing men who tear me down.

Being comfortable with my body is the first step towards healing and opening up to others. My fat has sheltered me from fingers that tickle (from "the shell") and even though I know now that I was molested, I try not to see it as a total negative. I was a victim as a child, but I don't have to remain one.

I am now able to see how food and body image have separated me from people and feelings. That is why I am hoping to continue feeling and exploring. I don't want not to be touched. I want to feel alive and connected to my body, my feelings and hopefully someday, a sensitive partner who will love me as much as I am capable of loving myself.

Photo: Ken Handler

Me at 16 with my first love.

He Loves Me,
He Loves Me Not

Scared to Death

You ask me why I resist you,
close myself off from your embrace,
shut down when you turn on.

To tell you the truth,
I'm scared to death,
scared that you don't know me,
that you love only who you think I am.

What if I told you
that I was once quite heavy,
that jeans wouldn't fit me,
that my belly held enough fat for two people?

You see me looking sexy,
your hands all over my sleek body.
You lift me up so easily,
carry me with grace to the bed.

What if one day you couldn't lift me anymore,
if I were to regress,
become just plump old me again?

Would you still like me,
want me,
admire me,

or would you leave me,
ashamed to show me to your friends?

Maybe I should gain a few—
test you?

To tell you the truth,
that scares me more.
What if you fail the test,
walk out the door,
not want me anymore?

It Doesn't Replace

Another bite of chocolate,
potato chips,
down to my last bag:
        It doesn't replace
        the best night I ever had.

Milk Duds,
popcorn at the show,
butter on my fingers:
        It doesn't replace
        the man that still lingers.

Cheeseburgers,
French fries;
Mother's homemade cheesecake
        doesn't begin to dull
        the sound of my heartbreak.

Chili dogs,
cotton candy,
amusement park shows
        don't erase the memory
        of him biting my toes.

Breakfast for the taking,
eggs and bacon,
sticky French toast
        don't change the fact
        that we can only wave from Coast to Coast.

Thick juicy lobster,
clams on the half shell,
Caesar salad
        don't erase the pain
        of a lost love ballad.

If I send him a box of chocolate
with half of it gone,
completely digested,
        with a note saying, "I LOVE YOU,"
        will I be rejected?

First an apple,
then an orange,
a ripe juicy apricot
        can't stop this crazy carousel:
        He loves me, he loves me not.

Mirror Madness

I really loved him. He was everything to me. His name was Matt, and it was as if being with him had finally filled the hole that was inside me. It had been over a month since we had spoken. Our relationship just sort of ended, with no real closure, and closure has always been very important to me.

Without closure I eat. I brood. I become tied up in knots, and angry. Anger is a major cause of self-abuse. I remember missing him so badly that I found myself standing naked in front of my bathroom mirror. Suddenly, it wasn't about him anymore—it was about me. Before I knew what had happened, the words started coming out of my mouth like a repressed storm.

"You fat, ugly bitch! You stupid woman! So stupid! You are fat and worth nothing! You are a failure! You stupid body! You think you can be fat and get away with it? You think you can run my life? Well, I'll show you!"

I had begun pinching my belly, and imagined myself sawing it off. I hurt myself by verbally abusing my body and ripping into it like nothing I had ever seen. It was as if I were watching myself from a spectator's seat. I felt numb and didn't understand why I was so mad at my body. Matt loved my body. I even loved my body sometimes. What was happening?

I only ate once a day for two weeks after that, and once again became obsessed with food because I was nearly starving myself during the day. I felt like a failure, and that if I could become thin, I would be successful. That was the mixed-up logic that I believed. Well, I didn't fail—Matt failed me. He took from me and then walked away when he was finished.

I needed to love somebody, so I let myself love him. I let love make me feel like I was nothing, but if I had been nothing, then he wouldn't have fallen in love with me and felt so overpowered by his feelings that he had to run away. I moved him and gave him all of myself, unselfishly and completely.

My body bore the brunt of my anger, and love became just the weapon my anger needed. Well, I have disarmed myself and am trying to live by the lessons of my body and spirit, and hopefully one day they will let me love again. The body can get in the way of love, but the path to loving oneself is the path out of the way to love.

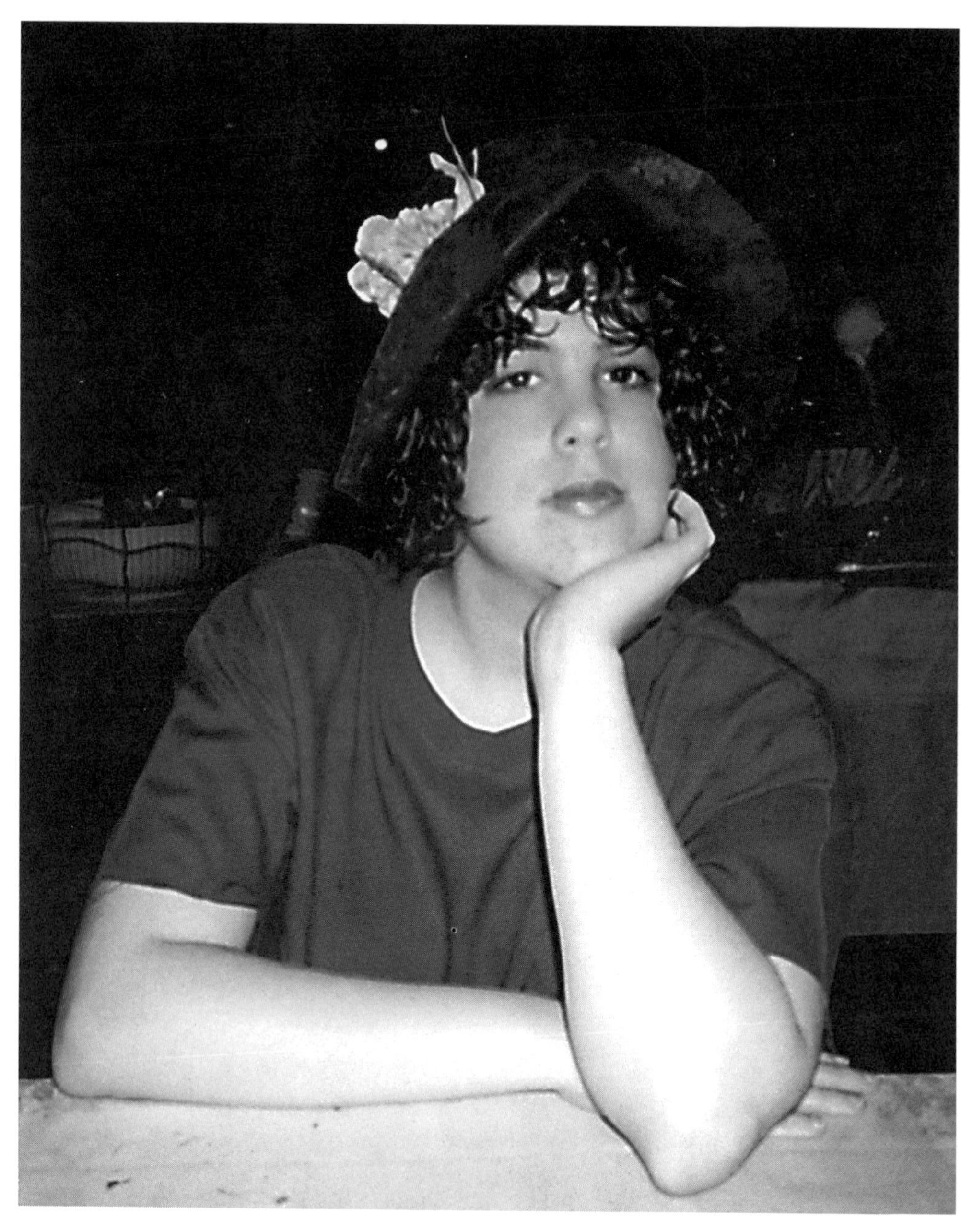

Enjoying the success of yet another
liquid diet, 1991—155 pounds.

The Power

I walk down the street
feeling the power—
alive again.

My body is slender;
it's a brand-new person
staring at me in the mirror.

I hear the whistles,
the gasps of awe;
it makes me feel the power.

I can have any man I want,
be anything,
become a goddess.

So why am I so scared,
hiding sometimes
behind blush and dark glasses?

Can't anybody see
it's still me,
shy and sometimes unsure?

Sometimes it's overwhelming,
being a woman,
being attractive.
I am afraid.

The power of a woman is now mine.
Am I truly myself for the first time,
or was this power always in me
even when I was chunky?

Control

As it enters my mouth
tasting so delicious,
filling my tummy
I feel truly full.

I have complete control
as the food enters me,
unlike when you entered me
and I became a baby.

I was helpless,
vulnerable to you in countless ways.
Now I eat to bury myself
underneath clothes that hide what you ravished.

I stick it in the microwave;
you stuck it in me.
Control was nowhere in sight
as you titillated me with delight.

If I stopped my splurge,
took a moment to breathe,
would I still be able to run
far enough away

or would the power be yours
to open all my locked doors,
see what I shove down inside,
possibly hurt me?

No, I must eat away the fear,
the part of myself you held near
until she cannot be found
even by me.

She is wild, possibly in love;
she scares me.
If she opens her mouth to speak,
she might scare you too.

So shut her mouth with food
to keep us both safe
if only for a moment
in this world of lost control.

Yummy!

Just an Empty Space

Here I am again,
drowning in my own consumption,
trying to fill the gap
that you briefly filled with your splendor.

Just an empty space in my bed
where you watched me fall in love.
Now you are gone
and I am hungry.

Kitchen cabinets try to compensate
for the empty cabinets of my heart.
They are bare
and I am left alone to restock.

Please come back and hold me!
Food can only sustain my stomach.
My heart is starving;
only you can feed it.

I want to tell you how much I love you,
and how meaningless this food really is,
after having really been fed
with only memories as leftovers.

Oversexed and Underfed

Alone I sit with an aching gut,
feeling overstuffed
and slightly like a slut.

Tears are my beverage,
food my savior.
Oversexed and underfed,
pretending to make myself full
while inside I feel empty and dead.

The phone is silent.
I try to fill the hole.
Being fat again
will give me back control.

If I become huge,
this lost lonely blob,
who would want me anyway?

No more one-night stands,
loss of control,
use of my curvaceous body,
devouring of my soul.

I guess I've never felt quite so used—
yet in a strange way attractive—
because sex, like food,
makes me emotionally reactive
and, like food,
I always want more.

Another Food Masquerade

I sat there tonight in front of the television. I was a hungry animal, stuffing down two Big Macs and two orders of fries. It was over in less than an hour. I couldn't believe it. What was I doing and what could have possibly been the reason for such gluttony?

Well, this book is becoming more and more about my own personal answers and questions. It may be too late tonight to stop my splurge, but I did become aware of something this week that, if dealt with, could be the key to preventing this from happening as often as it does.

Having been introduced to such intense physical touch at a young age, I believe that my needs have been much more intense even as an adult. I am a woman with extreme physical needs. It isn't so much the sex, as it is touching and fondling, as well as role playing and fantasizing.

I eat to cover the frustration of lack of touch as well as to make myself feel less sexual. How sexual can I feel after eating so much junk? It can get very hard to live with, the continuous need to have my body explored and pleasured.

I do know that my feelings are okay and normal. We all need love and touch. I think *love* is the word that should be explored here. The truth is, I want to be loved; and because touch hasn't always involved love for me, I seem to be even more hungry for true, unconditional love and devotion.

I have so much love inside that I honestly feel like I am dying sometimes. I used to cry to relieve my body of the pain and emptiness. I have a lot of trouble crying these days. The food doesn't let me cry. It shelters me so much that I sometimes can't even feel my pulse after I have binged.

Well, tonight I feel my pulse, despite my food masquerade. The party is over. I am unmasked and very afraid. There is somebody that I need to talk to and this person is away from me where he cannot be reached.

When I express myself fully, I feel alive and food loses its grip on me. Few people can handle my honesty and candor, yet this person lets me express myself. Yes, he is a man, and men are and have been a great source of frustration for women, especially women who need so much and end up crashing into that brick wall that men hide behind.

I am not ashamed of loving and needing men. I only wish to say that it is when I have lost myself to a man, to the point of no return, that I have felt disappointed in myself. But wanting and needing to be held and loved is certainly nothing to be ashamed of. If I stop stuffing myself with phony comfort, I will probably find love a lot more accessible.

It is painful, wanting to tell this man my feelings and desires. I ache inside to the point of insomnia and stomach cramps. I have always felt everything in my stomach, every emotional pain, every love pain, joy, sorrow, stage fright and just plain aliveness. Isn't it interesting how the stomach is where food goes and that all my feelings center right in the area that food camouflages?

It is very humbling to surrender feelings to a man who can at any moment take what he learns and use it as ammunition for control. Men tend to do that around powerful women, and he is terrified of my power. I am terrified of my power. Sometimes I hate him for making me feel so much, because now I can't go back. I am here, in this new place of truth and discovery. Hating him would be too easy. In order to keep the food from winning, I have to face him and not hold myself back anymore, and if that means telling him a thing or two, so be it. What will come of this situation, I do not know. I just know that food almost suffocated me tonight and I can't allow myself not to feel and breathe in the depth of my aliveness.

I know that all of this illumination has been inside me all along, and that no other person truly opened me up to my personal truth. A man happened to be the catalyst to a lot of hidden answers inside of me, but ultimately I am the ringbearer for the hidden diamond within; that is really something only I can choose to find and bring out from its not-so-tiny black box.

I feel very out of control and very scared, but the point is, I'm feeling. Control is sometimes lost to me when it comes to men, but I am not lost to me. I am in control of my thoughts and it is not "food for thought," it is "feeling for thought."

Personal Reflection

Marriage and Mourning

I was walking down the aisle, realizing that something was missing. Where was my father? Why was my grandfather walking me down the aisle?

It suddenly hit me. My father had died the night before, vanished right before my very eyes, on the night before what was supposed to be the most beautiful day of my life. There was a hole inside me that I had already tried to fill for months, by eating and eating and eating.

So, there I was, 210 pounds, without my figure, without my father, and getting blindly married in hopes of being saved.

Well, the marriage didn't save me, the food didn't save me, and my father died anyway. The eating didn't stop him from dying and it can't bring me any closer to him now. It didn't stop the funeral that we had to go to the next day. Life took over with death and I had to live through that death without disappearing myself. The food kept me dead inside, and I had to eat a little less and cry a little more before I could see daylight again.

I have saved myself by not eating myself to death and by being with the family that I do have and love very much. I try to live for what I have, rather than eating for what I don't.

At 200 pounds, 1994

Wed and Weighted

James and I had only been married one month. It had already begun, the subtle hints and the never-ending dread of once again not fitting the size. Only this time, it wasn't my grandmother pressuring me to lose weight. It was my mother-in-law, Deidre.

I remember how she took my sister-in-law Laura and me out to lunch at this hip, midtown restaurant. We had no sooner ordered when she ever-so-sweetly suggested that we all go to see Lorraine, this nutritionist that Deidre swore by. I could tag along with her and her thin daughter as they rearranged their eating habits, and if by some chance I wanted to, I could get the support I needed for my oh-so-obvious problems with food.

I didn't want to appear rude, so I agreed. As it turns out, Lorraine and I had already met. I had gone to see her a year earlier. I thought she was terrific then, and thought it was fate that Deidre and I had been going to the same nutritionist. Perhaps I was meant to return.

She was still just as terrific, and I still see her to this day. However, those days of mixed-up meals and my meddlesome mother-in-law were enough to make me crazy. As Deidre and I waited for Laura in Lorraine's waiting room, the conversation centered around how loved ones can never let the people they love hurt themselves. As subtle as she was trying to be, I got the message.

As hard as she tried to make it appear she really cared about me, it became apparent over the next two years that it was only her son she cared about. In her judgmental eyes, I was too fat and unhealthy for him. My diabetes was now to be monitored by my new-found family. They discussed everything: what doctor I should go to, how often, and what foods were downright dangerous for me. I felt invaded and angry.

James' verbal abuse continued behind closed doors. He criticized my dead father, while his mother was very much alive and running her son's angry mind. My father couldn't defend himself, but God forbid I should say anything negative about his mother. He would talk, time and time again, about how my father hadn't raised me right. After all, my father never went to synagogue, and James definitely thought my parents should have forced me to go. He kept commenting negatively on my father's unique qualities, and said that my father had never worked a day in his life.

My father was a self-educated, self-made man of great independence and creativity. He dabbled in a great many things, such as photography, real estate, and filmmaking. He wrote music and played both the piano and harpsichord.

He was free to be everything that James could only wish he could be. James was stuck in a world where he felt he had to please his parents and not disappoint them. Disappointing them scared him more than anything, so he lived in his own angry world, where he took me as his prisoner.

He would quiz me on math in the middle of a romantic dinner, knowing very well that math wasn't my best subject. He felt that I did not really have learning disabilities, and that I had been coddled through school. He believed that I was unsuccessful, that I had too many fears; I had to get over my fear of flying and my fear of lightning. I had to change who I was, and once again fit the size and the lifestyle that his family deemed appropriate.

This had all started before we got married, but I was so sick with grief over my father's death that I would have married a poisonous snake if it could have offered me some security. The deadly bite would have tickled compared to the pain I was feeling. Well, I was poisoned.

I was poisoned mentally, as I watched all my self-confidence and self-esteem slip away. As I sat there crying in Lorraine's office, I knew I had made a mistake. Deidre had spent the entire time in that waiting room telling me how I needed to change and what was unacceptable to their family. She never said it in so many words. Everything was so sweetly toned and colored, all wrapped up in a box that would eventually become my prison.

I was trapped, locked up in a marriage where little pieces of me were chipped away, until they were all over the floor for everyone who really loved me to sweep up. My mother had to watch as I doubted myself and my life. My family watched as James made me feel terrible about my weight, my learning disabilities, and my life as an artist. If only I could get a real career, like his mother and sister. That was really Deidre talking, but James became her abusive messenger.

When Deidre thought I was eating too many French fries, I would hear about it. If I needed to lose more weight, I would hear it ringing so loudly in my ears that I was almost deafened by Deidre's overbearing voice. I was constantly trying to be something that I wasn't.

We had to go to his family's synagogue. It didn't matter that we were married and needed to find our own place of prayer together. Nobody asked me what I thought about anything. I was just expected to conform to his same rigid family ways—to become thin, healthy, professional, conservatively-dressed Stacey.

Eventually, I confronted Deidre and asked her not to pressure me anymore, that I liked myself the way I was. She took it to mean I didn't want her love anymore, but love to her was the same as smothering. If she couldn't rule her children's lives, then they were pushing away her love. She said she would do it my way and back off, but that I would regret it. She implied that once somebody rejected her kind of love, they never got back in the door.

Well, she went right to her son and threw him in the middle. I had promised James that I would not put him in the middle, between his mother and me. But he wanted to be in the middle. Once again, he had to prove his love for his mother by putting me down and saying that she was right, and that I blew it.

I guess that, when one finally opens one's mouth after years of silence, they risk "blowing it." I risked becoming an outcast of a narrow-minded family and I don't regret one moment of it.

James and I had started to drift apart. I was going to nightly poetry readings while he was having dinner with his family a couple of nights a week. One night, I came home feeling happy and successful. James walked in, told me about his dinner, then brought up his mother. I knew trouble was coming.

His mother had wanted to know when I was planning on losing the weight. The same old song, but not the same old response. I picked up the phone and dialed his mother's number. Deidre answered and I asked her for a special favor. I asked her if she could please come to me directly about any problems she had with me, instead of going to her son and putting him in the middle of everything. I hung up and looked over at James, whose jaw had nearly hit the floor.

Once he got over his initial shock, he demanded I apologize to his mother or our marriage was over. He had threatened divorce constantly. Before we were married, he threatened to break up with me if I didn't go snorkeling with him, and if I wouldn't stop acting childish when I was so terrified on the ski slopes the first time I ever went skiing.

I did eventually apologize for hanging up on his mother, but not for what I said. I meant everything I said. I really shouldn't have apologized for hanging up, but I guess I still had the slightest bit of hope that our marriage might be saved. James had some wonderful qualities, and I had hoped that his good qualities would outweigh the abuse. Unfortunately, the man I had fallen in love with was lost to an overbearing family and anger that he could never properly express.

One night, after I was told once again that I would amount to nothing and that the book I was working on was crap, I told James to go to his birthday dinner without me. He looked embarrassed by the thought of showing up at his own birthday dinner wifeless, but I didn't care. I had been embarrassed, humiliated, and totally cut down by him so many times, I felt it was his turn to feel like something was missing. It was time for him to be without the woman whom he claimed to love, and yet tore apart until she had nothing left to give him.

It was time for me to give to myself. When he got

home that night, I was gone. I slept on my sister's floor that night with her cats crawling on my back. When I realized that I was getting more acknowledgment from those cats than I had gotten from my husband in months, I knew it was useless to continue being his wife. I needed to be me.

His mother made all the demands in the divorce and James went along with whatever she wanted. I was just thrilled to be rid of the both of them and free to find myself somewhere in the mess that James and his family had made of me.

One thing I can say: Divorce was the beginning of my life, not the end of love. I am stronger, better, and—most importantly—no longer lost in silence. Even the eating and body image disorders have taught me about life and love. The clarity that has come into my life has been from the victory of my own survival and the recognition of my own inner strength.

The one thing that has changed is my outlook on life. But it has changed because I found my own hidden voice, and had the courage to leave a bad marriage before it had the chance to destroy me. I needed to go through the marriage and the ketosis to realize that my life is important and not something that should be thrown away.

There is nothing more difficult than the loss of self. But when you clear out all the debris, you are still in there somewhere, and when you find yourself again in a whole new light, there is nothing more rewarding.

My family at my grandparents' 58th Wedding Anniversary. Left to right: myself, my sister Samantha, Grandmother Ruth, my brother Jeff, and my mother Suzie.

My Grandpa Elliot and me, 1993.

My parents
Ken (painted by Elliot) and Suzie.

My parents in 1985.

Below,
my grandmother
(Mother's mom)
and me, 1987.

My parents and me in Europe, 1991.

The Real "Ken"

I can tell you what the real Ken was like, what kind of life he led and what kind of woman he loved. My father and I were very close and I loved having him as my father.

The real Ken was a Renaissance man. He sat for hours playing away at his harpsichord and piano. We were similar in the way we listened to our music in solitude. My father knew every Verdi opera, and every other opera, for that matter. When he was young, all the other kids were listening to the latest sensation while my father listened to and learned probably close to every classical music piece there was.

My father had a dark beard, which he let grow very long in his later years. He looked so much like Verdi that when we visited Verdi's hometown in Italy, everybody thought that my father was Verdi reincarnated. My father loved taking us through Europe and was very knowledgeable about the art, music and culture.

He took beautiful photographs. He would go all over New York City with his camera around his neck. He would have it close to his chest and wouldn't even need to look into the lens to catch one of those moments. He would just click away and, most of the time, nobody was the wiser. He went to neighborhoods where violence was an everyday occurrence. He risked his life on several occasions when he let his camera catch drug deals, brutality and gang-related incidents.

He loved to help inner city kids and would go out of his way to get them the right legal and emotional support. He understood about lives that were less fortunate than his own and he taught his family about compassion. Sometimes he would help people, to his own detriment. One person he tried to help stole my mother's good silver and another one threatened our family.

His intentions were always wonderful and it wasn't always easy to watch the disappointment in his eyes when one of his inner-city youngsters fell short of his hopeful expectations. Nonetheless, he continued his projects, one of which was a break dance movie that he wrote and directed in the mid-eighties. It was called "Delivery Boys" and is available in some small specialty video stores.

He experimented with many different types of music in his life and had his own record label in the sixties. Sometimes it was hard to get him to listen to anything other than what he was obsessed with at the time. Since music was so important to me growing up, that could be difficult for me to deal with. When he didn't take an interest in my music, I would eat out of frustration.

For a while he was my manager in the music business. He traveled to Minneapolis with me, where I sang and wrote songs with J. D. Steele and his family. They are a well-known gospel family in Minneapolis; and working with them gave me soul and a sense of what I could really do with my voice. We ended up doing Minneapolis funk and recorded some stuff at Paisley Park, Prince's recording studio.

When I wanted to break out into other kinds of music, my father didn't want to help me. We battled and fought about music and what I should and shouldn't be doing musically. That would also cause me to overeat. The music business wasn't ready for me at that time. Since I wasn't a dancer, and good voices were becoming less and less important, I gave up. I just didn't have the look and the image. I thought for sure that the music business would reject me because I wasn't thin, so I began pursuing other things. Just another thing my body image got in the way of.

Now about the woman my father fell for and married when he was nineteen. He told me that when he first saw my mother's knees, he knew she was the one. She wore those cute white bobby socks and had beautiful golden yellow-blonde hair. She couldn't stand him at first. It was a blind date. They ended up meeting again a few years later, and, this time the fireworks were there for my mother as well.

Now, my mother is blonde in a way Barbie could only dream of. She is also a real woman. While "Ken" the doll was courting Barbie at beach parties, my father, the real Ken, was enjoying his life with his full-figured true love, my mother.

They enjoyed renovating old houses and traveling through Europe together. Their relationship was solid and special. He accepted her the way she was and they both gained weight together while enjoying frozen Sara Lee desserts. It was part of the contentment of a new marriage.

Over the years, he loved her even more. He never expected her to be thin enough to wear his mother's clothes, even though she was offered them by my grandmother. My grandfather once implied that if only she would lose weight, she would have the privilege of wearing Ruth's clothes.

My father once told me that he wouldn't want my mother to change for anything in the world. He recognized the shallowness that society sometimes exhibited.

He helped me to realize that men looked at me all the time, even though I had a butt. He told me that Latin men especially would kill to go out with me.

Well, since my first love was Latin, I understood what he meant. Spanish men loved me, and I like them, too. Because of my parent's influence, I was very open-minded, and therefore I attracted men who were open-minded about full-figured women.

Since losing my father, I have forgotten how to love myself. My life has become less secure, therefore triggering terrible eating patterns. I trust food not to leave me and I can control how much disappears inside my arteries. If I want to fill myself completely, I have the resources. McDonald's delivers, and so do so many places. In Manhattan, a food fix is just a phone call away, any time of day or night.

My father is out of my reach, but food is always there. Once somebody loses one parent, the fear of losing the other one becomes much more real. I have had a lot of death in my life, and feel helpless in the face of all this loss and turmoil. I have lost three people I love in a five-year period, and loss like that has totally pulled the rug out from under me.

My father was such a strong part of my world that now, I feel weak, in a world that I sometimes can't even understand. It is difficult to understand loss and to come to the realization that we really have very little control as mere mortals in this world.

Since control or lack of it is what causes eating disorders, it becomes apparent why there are so many desperate attempts to gain control with food. Well, food ends up controlling us and that is unfortunate.

Remembering my father alive and in his true glory has helped me to understand my loss more. For so long I could only think of that horrible night before my wedding, when my father lay on his deathbed. I could only remember how his body started to get cold, while I was having a family dinner at the Four Seasons Restaurant. We received a call that he was beginning to leave us, and we all jumped up from the table and ran to get to him in time to say goodbye.

It was horrifying to enter our home, not knowing whether he would be dead or alive. We made it in time. The rest of the night was just plain indescribable. In the Jewish religion, if there is a wedding and a funeral, the wedding must go on first. That is exactly what happened.

For so long, that was all I could focus on, the wedding, the funeral and how my life became such a blur. It has taken me five years to unblur my life and to find myself somewhere in it.

I want the world to know that the real "KEN" was a wonderful man and that, even though he wasn't perfect, he was my dream father. My mother and I are very close and I treasure every day we have together.

I have much love to give and it is that love that helps me to take better care of myself. I still struggle with food and self-love, but now that I realize that perfection is a myth, I cut myself enough slack to get by. Being human is okay, even though it is not always easy.

When I lost my dog Max, I lost myself to ketosis once again. I wanted control back. Love is not about control and unfortunately, neither is death.

Grandma Ruth and me in New York City, 1980.

Me with my dad.

Courtesy of Ruth Handler Photo: Allen Grant

My grandparents with Barbie.

Elliot Handler

Not All Women

Elliot Handler

Not All Women

Not all men reject
the women shallow men ignore.
Not all women should be thin;
sometimes better means more.

Women need not suffer,
starve themselves to the moon;
not all men want to hear about the diet
that fails all too soon.

Not all people stay the same
as they thicken with age;
beauty and perfect figures get smudged
like ink on a page.

Little girls should be happy,
should not have to doubt their own reflection,
grow up to be women
to deal with society's rejection.

Teenage girls shouldn't have to get hurt
trying to get that perfect figure,
wondering, if they don't get thinner,
will they be loved less bigger?

Not all women are the same.
They shouldn’t have to lose this dangerous game,
pay the price
of society’s fame.

Fat I Am

I am but a blob;
I like butter,
not margarine,
with my corn on the cob.

I am a heap of waste
taking society's garbage.
It is only food I taste
as I am pushed aside with such cruel haste.

I am fat,
fat I am.
I want my cholesterol
my green eggs and ham.

I will not be told
that I will not make it,
die before I am old,
that only the fat die young.

I will not wither away,
measure myself by cellulite loss,
be pasted on a bus,
skinny and starving at any cost.

I am famous
for having a loving heart.
Though full of hardened animal fat,
harsh words will never tear it apart.

Sunny Side Up on a Nude Beach (A Man's Perspective)

I watch you secretly through binoculars
lying sunny side up in the Florida sun.
I wonder if you know my eyes are in awe
of how beautiful you are,

your voluptuous curves,
your confident nudity
alongside many other bodies,
most of them starved
in one way or another.

You lie there in your own special world
unaffected by the herd of public perfection
surrounding you like a tropical storm.

Sunny side up,
your breasts golden yolks in the sun.
Larger than life they glisten!
My tongue, the fork that wants to dig in.

Your tummy moves like the sea,
big and full,
beautiful like a Titian or Rubens painting.
If I could paint you, I would.

If only I could come down to where you are,
tell you of your beauty
without embarrassing you—
without embarrassing myself.

My friends wait for me by the sea;
I see them smirking behind their shades.
I wonder if you really are unaffected,
if you cannot see them pointing,
acting so immaturely.

I wonder why they are unaffected
by such a classic beauty
showing her large body to the world,
a world that frowns upon squeezable flesh.

Time to meet the guys,
erected and lost
in a world of slender thighs.
I am erect and lost
in your eyes and your smile.

As I get closer
to my beauty queen
sunny side up in the sun
(my friends having their fun)
I want to hold you,

just to touch your hair
long and fluffy down your thighs,
if only I could.

I lie next to you,
just to whisper that you are special.
It was worth it
just to see your smile.

I hold your hand in the sand
where nobody can see
that it is wet with tears.

To Those Eyes That Criticize

Photo: Ken Handler

1975—Me holding my baby brother.

Just a Child

I

When a child becomes an adult,
the child still lingers
remembering the times of criticism,
unkind slaps to the self-esteem.

The child that is told unloving things
is denied of self-love
and, without love of self,
is in danger of starving in more ways than one.

The child strives to please,
to become what is expected,
even when it is difficult
and sometimes impossible.

Just a child,
a gift to the universe,
suddenly plays dangerous games
to win what they believe will win them love.

Love becomes perfection.
Perfection does not exist.
So where does that leave love;
where does that leave the children of tomorrow?

II

You finally accepted me,
told me I could be heavy and still okay.
I could say it's fifteen years too late,
but I love you, and I know you love me.

I have been thin,
I have been fat;
you have loved me through it all.
If only you would have accepted me
when I needed acceptance.

Even as an adult,
I became that helpless child
at family dinners
in front of friends,
where you spoke in loud voices
about my habits and food choices.

I became just a fixture on the wall
in all your dark dining rooms of scrutiny.

III

I tried so hard to be like the other girls on the beach,
to properly pour on my sunscreen,
to be that unreal beauty.
Only, I am real.

Can you deal with real,
the sadness that, as a child,
you made me feel
the woman that I am now?

You never heard the cries for acceptance.
If you are listening now,
if you still hear a child's voice,
it is because I am just a child grown up
with a voice that could never quite reach you.

Trying to be that perfect bathing beauty—173 pounds.

Steven Cavallo

Through the Eyes of You

I have finally succeeded!
I am thin now.
Can you see my rib cage
becoming more and more apparent?

I don't care about stuff anymore,
only about being thin,
not caring how,
only about getting there.

If only losing my fat
could help me lose my pain.
Now I am obsessive,
vain and insane.

Insanity is vanity;
the reverse holds true.
I've tried to become myself
through the eyes of you.

My feelings are trapped inside,
hidden from you for so many years.
Stripped of my fat,
there is no longer a place to hide my tears.

1980

"Lose Some Weight and I'll Buy You the Store"

You told me in the dressing room,
"Lose some weight and I'll buy you the store."
And when I told you I lost thirty pounds,
you said, "Lose thirty more."

No matter what I did,
nothing was ever enough.
You made looking in the mirror
so very tough.

Even when you were not so tactful,
I believe you wanted to help me;
you had your own vision of beauty,
your own skinny reality.

You always told me I could lose more weight
and, now that I've been as thin as I could be,
I've had to face my own reality:
that thin may just not be me.

My grandmother and me, "Just another meal."

According to Plan

I know it did not go according to plan,
that I botched things up
by being the thirteen-year-old plump child
who suffered in every dressing room,
trying to fit your idealized size.

I always wanted to be perfect in your eyes.
Imagine my disappointment
when your perfection became a locked door,
one I never had the key for.

I guess I finally came to the conclusion
that my perfection needs a bigger keyhole
with more room to breathe
and is altogether behind a different door,

and that God granted me a beautiful body,
just not a perfect one.
He created me with average hips,
larger bones,
and a baby face with cheeks that are squeezable.

He gave me challenges,
those difficulties that the perfect doll never faces;
so perfect I guess I am not.
Is anybody?

Personal Reflection

Forgiveness

It is almost time for me to conclude this journey of words and feelings. I think that one of the most important lessons I've learned is that love is difficult. Whether it is love of self, or love of another human being, it is difficult and stormy along the way.

I have to say that silence is very painful for me, especially when the release of feelings has been so essential to helping me find my hidden voice, and to conquer a lot of deep-rooted issues. I believe that when something deep inside needs to be resolved, and another person is involved, it is necessary to work things out with that other person. Unfortunately, that other person may not want it resolved; then it becomes just you and your "stuff."

The truth is, it is up to each individual to heal himself. I have been struggling and working to heal myself for several years now. It takes time and perseverance, and nobody can do it for you.

About two years ago, I had a falling out with a relative. I bore the brunt of this person's anger and hostility. I could not defend myself at the time, because this person behaved so irrationally that it took me several minutes to even begin to comprehend behavior so mean and selfish. Essentially, this person tore me down in public. It was an evening that was supposed to be enjoyable, but turned out to be unpleasant and humiliating.

There was nobody I could talk to about it. I felt totally alone around my own family. I sat there for the next three hours, getting smashed beyond belief. I was scared because I rarely drink, and I felt as though I was fading away into some other realm where I couldn't find myself anymore.

The rest of the evening, I sat in my hotel room, surrounded by bad feelings and white chocolate bar wrappers. I ate myself into a stupor. It was a very painful night. I wanted revenge. Eventually, I came to realize that my relative's behavior was a reflection on her. Somebody who could behave that way publicly towards another person, especially another family member, really must be suffering inside; once I realized that, I was able to begin healing from that night.

As we all know, loss of control is what can lead to so much pain and confusion. I felt as though I had lost all my control and so I turned to food for solace. As always, food became just an illusion and reality hurt like hell. I began to realize that it was okay to feel vulnerable and that humans can't always be in control of everything.

I also realized that *success* is the best revenge. I have succeeded by being able to express my feelings and share them with other people. Feelings are so important— and they are the key to communication.

It has been very difficult to share my feelings with certain important people in my life. They have been unable to hear me completely, and that is painful. But in the end, I am still speaking, healing and loving. I know that I am doing what is right for me and that I am on my way to a healthier and happier life.

We cannot change people. We can only help to guide them. I cannot change the person who rejects my excess body fat. I cannot change the abusive people in my life and make them apologize. I can, however, try to forgive them over time, and most importantly, stop wasting my time on those people who really have no place in my life.

Remember, life is precious and we have so little time. We should not waste our time allowing hurtful people into our own sacred space. Imagine an invisible circle around each individual that represents their lives and their feelings. When we allow too many negative influences into our circle, we are damaging our sacred space. We own our space and should be true to ourselves.

Abuse of any kind is like a cigarette hole being burned into sensitive human flesh. Sometimes we have no choice but to experience abuse, as I did from my relative and from my ex-husband. But that does not mean that we should allow those people and situations to take up any more time in our lives. If we choose to forgive, it is for our own emotional well-being. If we are to let people go, release them from our sacred space, forgiveness can be our best friend.

I want to conclude this reflection by saying, no matter what happens and whom you let into your personal world, please be true to yourself and never let anybody make you feel small. Be true, be honest and don't be afraid of your vulnerability. Admitting vulnerability will make you feel stronger and much more emotionally available to the people who truly love you the way you are.

Shattered Perfection

I am asking women everywhere to realize
that they do have a choice,
a voice
and a reason to rejoice.

Being human means being imperfect;
it means having some fat on our bodies.
It means being able to feel,
being able to look inside
to see what is real.

Steven Cavallo

Shattered Perfection

Is imperfection a mere word
or the glass on many warped mirrors?
Mirrors that shatter
perfection remaining in bits and pieces.

To understand perfection
must we understand the reflection,
and when it is shattered
will we cut ourselves with the truth?

What happens when we finally become perfect
only to realize something else is very wrong,
only to see the diet wasn't enough,
that life goes on imperfect?

Can we really ever find that place
where perfection truly exists
or, like an incomplete jigsaw puzzle,
will a piece still be missing?

Or is perfection a dream,
a fairy tale that won't come true?
And if it is only a dream
do we stay asleep forever?

Now that you have left me,
my dear sweet ketosis,
I am once again a woman
waterlogged,
round in the thighs,
back to my normal larger size.

Though I am not so large, I've been told,
I look in the mirror and grow cold.
This disorder is getting old.

Out of Control

Everything is moving
at its own pace,
in its own time,

and here I am spinning
out of control,
unable to move,
watching life in slow motion.

It is difficult to understand
the comings and goings of time,
how it sneaks up on us
only to pass us by again.

I wonder if it will always be this way,
so frightening,
so out of control.

Will it get easier,
or will I always feel like crying
like a part of me is lost,
like a part of me is dying?

Will food always be the answer
to the helplessness I feel
when I want something now
and can't have it?

Food is immediate;
it numbs all my pain,
my fears of striving in vain.

I don't want to hurt this way.
Perhaps anger would be better?

Anger is the knot
that twists inside my being
until I am out of control,
yet unable to lash out.

So I sit quietly
with a calm tension inside.
It settles in my vagina
where my legs tighten around it.

Then I just feel hungry,
once again the overeater,
the lazy aching child,
watching my body widen
and my heart diminish.

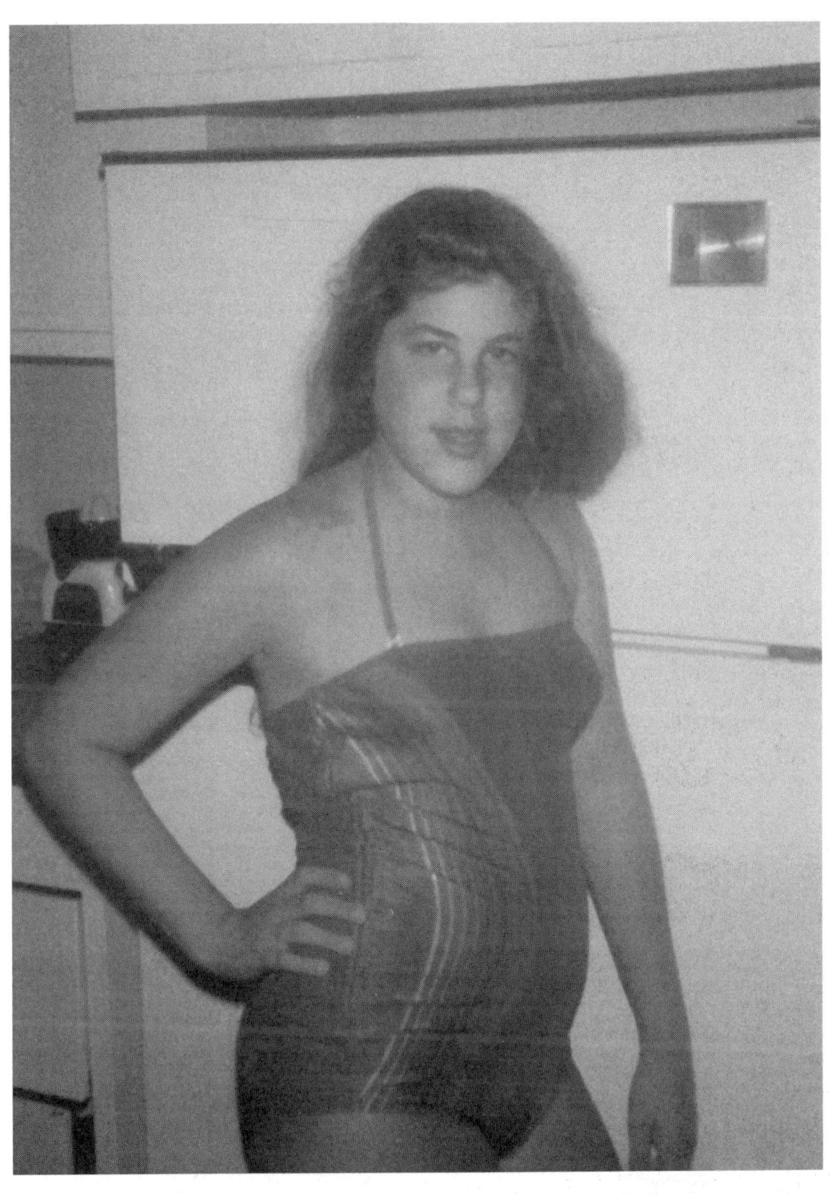

Twelve years old and beginning to "grow."

Photo: Samantha Handler

My Grandma Ruth, and me, 1999.

It Does Exist

The subject is not closed,
it has just begun.
It does exist;
ignoring it will not make it go away.

People are suffering every day,
trying to live up to unreal expectations,
and there have been very real consequences.

I wanted to be thin
no matter what,
and I would have died trying
but my own strength prevailed.

I am stronger than the warped mirror,
stronger than the image that has cast its shadow,
stronger than the criticism I have endured.
Many people have not been so strong;
some have died.

Too much time has been wasted on fantasy.
It is time to face the truth
that body image and eating disorders do exist
and will continue,
as long as love of the self
and the imperfect body
are nonexistent.

Don’t Lose Life

Photo: Acoy Cofiño

Don't Lose Life

If you decide to become thin,
to lose all those excess pounds,
don't stop caring about yourself;
don't lose life.

It's easy to go on a diet.
Living is the difficult part,
living with the real fears
instead of those reflected by the mirror.

What we see in the mirror
is only a small part of us.
It will not be our eternal success;
it should not be our failure.

When you feel out of control,
when your heart longs for washboard abs,
get back your control
by learning to work with what you have.

Being truly in shape
does not necessarily mean being thin.
Being thin
does not mean automatic health.

You cannot be perfect,
but even if you could,
being unhealthy is not only imperfect,
it is dangerous.

If you want to be thin,
for God's sake, be healthy!
If you want to be healthy
you don't have to be thin.

If you are heavier and happy with yourself,
then be happy.
If you love food,
enjoy yourself.

Whether you are thin or heavy,
don't hurt yourself
by starving,
purging,
searching for love behind the walls of food.

If you feel unloved,
being thin won't fix it;
if you can't love yourself unconditionally,
being thin won't lighten your load.

Lighten yourself
by loving yourself.
Self-acceptance is the key
that will truly unlock who you are.

The Roadblock

I

When you wake up in the morning
unable to face your own reflection,
when you cancel your plans
because you feel too fat,
that is when you know the problem is real.

When you can't get up from one single meal
without feeling like a blimp,
when you forget that feeling full is normal
and you feel guilty instead of satisfied,
you know the problem is getting worse.

When almost every waking hour
is spent thinking about your body,
how you want to change it—
how you cannot face life until you do—
the problem suddenly seems larger than life
and you feel suspended in frozen inner chaos.

When you miss a few days of exercise
and you punish yourself,
hiding under three sizes too large,
it is time to rethink things.

When you feel like a balloon
and cannot float away,
you wonder that if you could,
would God even accept you?

When you cannot accept yourself
naked,
in dress clothes,
on the beach,
in the arms of your lover,
in your own private hell,
there is no place to go but on a diet.

II

You live the diet;
it becomes your alter ego.
You fight it
needing desperately to accept it.

Every meal becomes an entanglement
of the hungry voices within,
starving to punish each other
yet needing to be fed.

III

When we are thrown off by life,
silenced by our own fears,
we feel out of control.

So to gain it back
we lose ourselves
to self-starvation,
overeating,
games of truth or dare,
where we always choose dare
and lose the truth.

The truth is the pain we feel,
the tears we need to let out,
the voices inside that make us special.

Whether we have starved ourselves
or locked ourselves up in excess fat,
we are special.

We are more than our bodies,
more than just a fashion statement.
We are a statement of humanity,
powerful enough to beat this roadblock,
whatever it is inside
that keeps us from being truly alive.

This book has been a personal journey, one that has started me on the road to a happier and healthier life. I still struggle with a body-image disorder, but feel more ready than ever to conquer it. I feel very close to anybody who has felt any of the feelings expressed in this book, and it has been a very special experience for me to have shared these feelings. I wish everybody who is reading this peace and happiness, and a chance at finding both from the place where they really exist: inside.